$3.00

Our First Estate

Our First Estate

The Doctrine of Man's Pre-Mortal Existence

R. Clayton Brough

INTERNATIONAL STANDARD BOOK NUMBER
0-88290-084-6

LIBRARY OF CONGRESS CATALOG CARD NUMBER
77-79753

Second Printing, May 1979

Printed in the
United States of America
by

**Horizon Publishers
& Distributors
P.O. Box 490
50 South 500 West
Bountiful, Utah 84010**

To

John, Madeline, Marsha-Lynne, and Robert.

Expression of Appreciation

The author would like to express sincere appreciation to Dr. Dale J. Stevens, Associate Professor of Geography at Brigham Young University, to Bishop Layne F. Blatter, Science Instructor at Springville Junior High School, and to Marilyn Groneman, Vocational Instructor at Springville Junior High School, for their insight and comments as to the doctrine contained within this book; and to Bryce C. Nelson, a Construction Engineer in Provo, and Ralph J. Snelson, Mathematics Instructor at Springville Junior High School, for their suggestions as to the title for this book; and to La Dore Goodsell, English Instructor at Springville Junior High School, for her review of this book and its grammatical content.

Also, deep thankfulness is expressed to Duane S. Crowther, President of Horizon Publishers, who expertly assisted this writer by making several doctrinal and organizational suggestions in reading this book for publication.

And last but most important, I am grateful to my lovely wife, Ethel, who has continually sustained, encouraged, and assisted me during my many hours of writing and revisions, and to the Lord, for His kindness in inspiring me in this research effort.

R. Clayton Brough

PREFACE

Ever since the human race began, man has asked himself the question "Where did I come from?" For an answer to that inquiry he has searched many sources. He has sought the divine inspiration of prophets, the imaginations of poets, the logic of philosophers, and even the skepticism of agnostics. However, today as in the past, the question of "Where did I come from?" still remains unanswered for most of mankind.

Yet, there is an answer to the question "Where did I come from?" That answer, along with other teachings dealing with "a life before this mortal life," may be found within the doctrines of The Church of Jesus Christ of Latter-day Saints, the only Christian religion today that still holds the belief of a "life before this life" as a fundamental doctrine. Relying upon the teachings of modern-day prophets and apostles and upon the principle of continuous revelation from God, Latter-day Saints hold it as common knowledge among themselves that every form of mortal life has had an existence before being born into this world. They call this "life before mortal life" the "pre-mortal existence," the "pre-earthly existence," or, as is often more simply but incorrectly expressed, the "pre-existence."

It is my intent to answer as fully as possible the questions "Where did I come from?" and even more importantly "Who am I?" that this book has been written. Using the scriptures and the inspired utterances and discourses of Latter-day Saint general authorities and other Church leaders, the author has tried to bring into focus the major events which transpired in our pre-mortal existence, and which ultimately affected our coming to this earth as spirit children of our Father in Heaven to inhabit a physical body of flesh and bones.

The reader should be aware that this is not an official Church publication and that this writer is solely responsible for the manner in which documented material is presented within this book. Therefore, it would be appropriate for those who read this book to seek inspiration from the Holy Ghost as to the truthfulness of the information contained herein, and apply that knowledge in such a way that righteousness will always prevail in their lives.

R. Clayton Brough

TABLE OF CONTENTS

CHAPTER ONE

The Evidence and Importance of Our "Pre-Mortal Existence"

Meaning of the Term "Pre-Mortal Existence"

Ever since the human race began, man has asked himself the question "Where did I come from?" For an answer to that query he has searched many sources. He has sought the divine inspiration of prophets, the imaginations of poets, the logic of philosophers, and even the skepticism of agnostics. However, today as in the past, the question of "Where did I come from?" still remains unanswered for most of mankind.

Yet, there is an answer to that searching question. That answer, along with other teachings dealing with "a life before this mortal life," may be found within the doctrines of The Church of Jesus Christ of Latter-day Saints, the only Christian religion today that still holds the belief of a "life before this life" as a fundamental doctrine. Relying upon the teachings of modern-day prophets and apostles, and upon the principle of continuous revelation from God, Latter-day Saints hold it as common knowledge among themselves that every form of mortal life has had an existence before being born into this world. They call this "life before mortal life" the "pre-mortal existence," the "pre-earthly existence," or, as is often more simply but incorrectly expressed, the "pre-existence."[1]

Concerning the usage of the terms "pre-mortal existence, pre-earthly existence, and pre-existence," Elder Daniel H. Ludlow, professor of ancient scriptures at Brigham Young University, has stated:

> The other word which appears to be somewhat misleading is used in connection with the soul or the spirit of man.

That word is pre-existence. I suspect that when this word is used we are really thinking of a pre-earthly existence, not of an existence of man before he actually existed, which, of course, would be a contradiction of terms.

Therefore, in discussing the subject of an earlier existence of man, I should like to use the terms "Pre-earthly existence [or pre-mortal existence]" rather than the traditional term of "pre-existence."[2]

This author agrees with Elder Ludlow, and will, therefore, use only the terms "pre-mortal" or "pre-earthly existence" when personally referring to the "life before this mortal life" throughout the rest of this book. All quotes by other individuals, however, will be left in their original forms.

Scriptural Evidence of a Pre-Mortal Existence

The belief of Latter-day Saints in a pre-mortal existence is principally based upon ancient and modern scripture, e.g.: the *Bible, Book of Mormon, Doctrine and Covenants,* and *Pearl of Great Price.* Elder William E. Berrett, former vice-president of religious education at Brigham Young University, has stated that "the scriptures are replete with revelations which not only establish the fact that we all lived before this earth life, but also add much knowledge concerning that existence."[3] In regard to this matter, Elder Daniel Ludlow has mentioned some of the most familiar Biblical scriptures that substantiate the belief by Latter-day Saints in a pre-mortal existence:

All of the major philosophies and religions of the world have attempted to find an answer to this important question [about our pre-mortal existence], but Christianity as it is taught in both the Old and the New Testaments, offers the most complete and most satisfactory answer of all. Although the teachings of the prophets as they are recorded in the present versions of the ancient scripture are not always as clear as many people would like them to be, yet I believe these prophets very clearly and definitely taught a pre-earthly existence....

Many of the earlier prophets were acquainted with the doctrine that we had an existence before this life as spiritual sons and daughters unto God. In Hebrews 12:9 Paul states: "Furthermore, we have had Fathers of our flesh which corrected us and we gave them reverence. Shall we not much rather be in subjection unto the Father of spirits and live?" Here Paul states that we all have a Father of our spirits.

In both of the 16th and the 27th chapters of Numbers, Moses refers to the "God of the spirits of all flesh." In Ecclesiastes 12:7 we read that the spirit will return unto God who gave it. How could a spirit return to God unless it had once been in the presence of God? Also, God told Jeremiah that he was chosen as a prophet in the spirit world before he ever came here upon this earth. In chapter one of his book, Jeremiah tells us, "Then the word of the Lord came unto me saying: Before I formed thee in the belly I knew thee; and before thou camest forth out of the womb I sanctified thee, and I ordained thee a prophet unto the nations."

Job also understood this doctrine. In the 38th chapter of his book he was asked by the Lord: "Where wast thou when I laid the foundations of the earth, when the morning stars sang together and the sons of God shouted for joy?" Notice in this verse that the sons of God existed before the earth existed in its present form. Also, notice the plurality of the term "sons."

Another indication that we all lived before we came upon this earth is found in the 32nd chapter of Deuteronomy, verses 7 and 8: "The Most High divided to the nations their inheritance; when he separated the sons of Adam he set the bounds of the people according to the number of children of Israel." Now how could God have known the number of the children of Israel before they ever appeared on the earth, unless they were in existence somewhere else at that time. This idea is substantiated further in Acts 17:27. Here we read that the Lord "hath made of one blood all nations of man and hath determined the times before appointed, and the bounds of their habitations." Thus, apparently God knew every person who was going to be born here upon this earth before that person was born on the earth. Paul summarizes these ideas in the 8th chapter of Romans where he says: "The spirit itself beareth witness with our spirit, that we are the children of God."

Perhaps the most striking scriptures of all on the doctrine of a pre-earthly existence, however, come from the teachings of the Savior in the New Testament. For example, you may recall this story as it is recorded in the 9th chapter of John: "And as Jesus passed by, he saw a man which was blind from birth, And his disciples asked him, saying: Master, who did sin, this man, or his parents, that he was born blind?" Jesus answered, "Neither this man sinned nor his parents; but that the works of God should be made manifest in him." (John 9:1-3) Notice the definite implication of a pre-earthly existence in both the question and the answer. If there were no such earlier life, the easiest and most obvious answer of the Savior would have been: "There is no existence before birth; therefore this man could not have sinned before he was born." However, the Savior made no such statement. Instead, he confirmed the belief of his disciples in an existence before birth by acknowledging that it was possible to commit sin before birth, but that this was not the case in the instance of this particular man.

On other instances, the Savior also taught that we are all sons and daughters of God. Did he not teach us to pray to our Father which art in heaven? Notice the use of the pronoun "our." Also, when the Savior appeared to Mary on the morning of his resurrection, he said to her: "Go to my brethren, and say unto them; I ascend unto my Father and unto your Father." (John 20:17) It is obvious here that Jesus Christ is saying that God is our Father in a sense that God is also his Father. That is, God is the Father of all of us as spiritual children. This is exemplified in those scriptures which refer to Jesus Christ as the "First born in the Spirit." If Jesus Christ were the only son of God in the spirit, then why the use of the adjective "first?"

Of course, the scriptures make it clear that Jesus has another Father-Son relationship with God that the rest of us do not have. God is the Father of the physical body of Jesus Christ as well as the Father of his spiritual body. Thus the scriptures correctly refer to Jesus as the "First born in the Spirit" but the "only begotten in the flesh."

What a wonderful message the Gospel has for us concerning our pre-earthly existence. We are all truly brothers and sisters—all the sons and daughters of divine parentage. This knowledge should help us understand one of the major purposes of life on this earth: to learn to walk by faith in an existence out of the presence of God where a veil is drawn over our eyes concerning our previous life with God. Thus we can gain a testimony of God by ourselves through faith rather than by sight. This truth of a pre-earthly life should also help us in our endeavors to love our neighbors as ourselves and to love God our Father with all our heart, mind, might, and strength. It is indeed one of the greatest truths that have ever been revealed to man.[4]

Other Biblical and modern-day scriptures that relate to and explain our pre-mortal existence will be quoted and commented on in later chapters within this book.

From the preceding Biblical passages quoted by Elder Ludlow, it is apparent that the Savior and his prophets and apostles of the Old and New Testaments knew, understood, and wrote about the doctrine of the pre-mortal existence. Why is it then that since the teachings of these men are contained in the Bible the majority of Christianity today does not accept the doctrine of a pre-mortal life? Elder Gary Ellsworth, a Latter-day Saint author, has written that the answer was "apostasy" from scriptural truths during and after the fall of the early Christian church:

> The doctrine of the pre-existence was an obscure idea for centuries between the time of the fall of the early church and the restoration of The Church of Jesus Christ of Latter-day Saints, which is the only Christian religion that still holds that belief as fundamental doctrine today. Yet, under the surface, there was enough philosophic speculation and poetic intuition to keep it alive.
>
> Wordsworth wasn't the only one who wrote about the pre-existence, but most Latter-day Saints are familiar with his lines:
>
> > *Our birth is but a sleep and a forgetting;*
> > *The Soul that rises with us, our life's Star,*
> > *Hath had elsewhere its setting,*
> > *And cometh from afar:*
> > *Not in entire forgetfulness,*
> > *And not in utter nakedness,*
> > *But trailing clouds of glory do we come*
> > *from God, who is our home....*
>
> (*"Ode* [*Intimations, of Immortality, from Recollections of Early Childhood*]", Wordsworth Poetry and Prose, *ed. W. W. Merchant, Cambridge, Mass., Harvard University Press, 1955, p. 577.*)
>
> Historians generally assume that the doctrine of the pre-existence was a Greek heresy that the Christian church

attempted to fight off. In fact, both the Greeks and the Christians learned it from the same divine source, the teachings of the Lord to the great patriarchs of the past. As people dispersed over the face of the earth, the concept of the pre-existence went with them, sometimes taking odd forms as time and myth altered the traditional teachings. As we would expect, the Old Testament prophets had a clear understanding of this important doctrine; for example, Jeremiah alludes to being ordained a prophet before his birth:

"Then the word of the Lord came unto me, saying,

"Before I formed thee in the belly I knew thee; and before thou camest forth out of the womb I sanctified thee, and I ordained thee a prophet unto the nations." (Jer. 1:4-5.)

The epistle to the Ephesians claims that "accordingly as he hath chosen us in him before the foundation of the world, that we should be holy and without blame before him in love." (Eph. 1:4.) This scripture shows an awareness of premortal callings.

After the apostasy, the doctrine of the pre-existence was taught by some early church leaders and condemned by others. Origen Adamantius, who lived in Alexandria about 185-254 A.D., was an active Christian who founded monastic orders and wrote epistles to nearly every area of the church. He believed in a premortal existence since it explained some of the diversities of mortal conditions:

"...Diversity was not the original condition of the creature, but that, owing to causes that have previously existed, a different office is prepared by the Creator for each one in proportion to the degree of his merit...." (*The Anti-Nicene Fathers,* ed. Alexander Roberts and James Donaldson, Grand Rapids, Michigan, William B. Eerdman Publishing Company, 1951, vol. 4, "Origin de Principiis," p. 292.)

Other Christian leaders who taught the doctrine in the first few centuries after the apostasy were Pierius, Justin Martyr, John of Jerusalem, and, to some extent, Augustine. Others were censured as the doctrine became more and more heretical, and finally teaching it was punishable by excommunication after Pope Justinian in 543 A.D. banned the doctrine by decree.

During the Renaissance and Reformation, as habits, customs, and traditions changed, the pre-existence idea surfaced again. Jacob Boehme (1575-1674), a shoemaker, philosopher, and great religious leader during the Reformation, felt that the soul had originated in places other than earth: "As the eye of man reaches the stars where...it had its primitive origin, so the soul penetrates and sees even within the divine state of being wherein he lives." (*The Doctrine of Jacob Boehme,* comp. Franz Hartman, New York, 1928, p. 52.)

For philosophers as well as for poets, the concept of pre-existence explained man as more than an animal and seemed to offer a key to the mysteries of the soul. Sir Oliver Lodge, noted English physicist, felt that the personality of man was the total experience of the soul both in this world and the world before:

"...We living men and women, while associated with this mortal organism, are ignorant of whatever experience our larger selves may have gone through in the past—yet when we wake out of this present materialized condition, and enter the region of larger consciousness, we may gradually realize...the wide range of knowledge which that larger entity must have accumulated since its intelligence and memory began." (*Science and Immortality,* Sir Oliver Lodge, New York, Moffat, Yard, and Company, 1910, p. 184.)

To many, it seems logical that a person's character is not simply the experience and knowledge of this world only. Those gifts, talents, and abilities may have been outgrowths of previous experience.

Furthermore, theologians found the doctrine of the pre-existence a more satisfactory answer to the problem of man's fallen nature than original sin, a teaching that robs God of the virtue of justice. John Wesley (1703-1791) and Edwin Beecher (1800-1888) argued against original sin by teaching that men were created in circumstances of "honor and right," but then "revolted and corrupted themselves, and forfeited their rights, and were introduced into this world under a dispensation of sovereignty, disclosing both justice and mercy...." (*The Conflict of Ages,* Boston, Phillips, Sampson & Company, 1854, p. 221.)

Beecher was closer to the truth, but was still in error. Earth life is a reward for our premortal obedience, not a punishment. We echo Thomas Traherne's inspired concept in the 17th century, that this world is a gift granted by a loving God to his child in the life before:

Long time before
I in my Mother's Womb was born,
A GOD preparing did this Glorious Store,

The World for me adorne.
Into this Eden so Divine and fair
So Wide and Bright, I come his Son and Heir.

("The Salutation," The Poetical Works of Thomas Traherne, *ed. Gladys I. Wade, London, P.J. & A. E. Dobell, 1932, p. 4.)* [5]

The Importance of Learning About Our Pre-Mortal Existence

As to why it is important or "significant" that a person strive to gain knowledge and understanding about the "Pre-mortal existence," Elder William E. Berrett has presented us with the following pertinent reasons:

What is the significance of the information that is available [on the pre-mortal existence of man]? The first significant result is that man is ennobled in our eyes. He is a God in embryo. He has been in the form of God from the beginning—from even before the foundations of the earth were laid. He is eternal. All men are brothers for the only foundation for a real brotherhood lies in the real Fatherhood of God. Personality is not solely the product of heredity and environment in this world. It is a complex product of an eternity of forces upon innate intelligence.

Secondly, this knowledge of a pre-earth period gives purpose to life. We are here to gain experience with the elements, to develop personality, to experience both joy and pain. The individual becomes the important unit. His importance transcends the importance of any political state or the perpetuity of any social organization.

The importance of understanding the purpose of life is realized when we examine the failure of science to discover any purpose at all....

The knowledge God has given us of our pre-earth life brings understanding to an otherwise dark world. It gives us understanding of man and his problems, it gives us a basis for understanding individual differences and helps us to realize why some intellects rise so far above others. It explains a Christ, a Beethoven, an Edison. We have long known that men are not born equal and now we understand why that is so. It brings to us such revolutionary information that in the fields of the social sciences we should lead the world.

Our knowledge of pre-earth life helps us to understand joy and pain, peace and war, good and evil and in the midst of life's gloomiest pages receive the assurance that all will yet be well. This knowledge warns us against the pitfalls of humanism and determinism. It gives the lie to the atheist. It brings us kinship with the God.[6]

In addition to the reasons which Elder Berrett has previously expressed, the Church has similarly published an article which states that through our understanding that "we lived for countless ages before we were born on this earth. . . as spirit beings. . . with our Eternal Father . . . ," we can come to recognize that "our life here" in mortality "is purposeful" and is "not by chance, but by design." The article reads as follows:

We lived for countless ages before we were born on this earth. This important truth, revealed anew, but only partially made known in the Bible, stands as one of the most meaningful doctrines restored in these last days. As spirit beings we lived with our Eternal Father where we were nurtured in principles of the gospel of Jesus Christ.

With this concept we are able to understand the purpose of our existence as well as our potential status as eternal beings. Born of Deity, we may reach the heights of godhood by obedience to the laws of progression.

We may also recognize that from the other side of the veil we have brought gifts and talents to be developed, acted upon, and used for the betterment of ourselves, our associates, and to advance the kingdom of God.

The truth is that our life here is purposeful; we are here not by chance but by design; consequently, we have a mission, foreordained, to become eternal mothers and eternal fathers, but only on conditions that we accept our responsibilities in this life as God has revealed them. The children born to us here are precious sons and daughters of God, lent to us that they might be strengthened in true principles to receive the opportunitiy to return home, having fulfilled the purpose of their creation.[7]

By gaining the knowledge and understanding that we existed before this earthly life, we are also helping ourselves to maintain a righteous and happy manner while here in mortality. In regard to this subject, President George Q. Cannon stated in 1884 the following:

> Now, if a man can only know whence he came, why he is here, and that which awaits him after this life, it seems to me that he has abundant causes of happiness within his grasp. Much of the unhappiness and uncertainty that prevail today in the minds of mankind arise from ignorance upon these points.... If a man knew exactly why God sent him here, the object that He had in giving unto him a mortal existence, do you think that men or women who had this knowledge would be guilty of suicide, would have any disposition to cut off their own existence and to destroy that gift which God in His mercy has given to us? I do not believe that any human being who properly comprehends the object that God has had in placing man here upon the earth, and who has a desire to carry out that purpose, would ever attempt self-destruction. He would shrink from such an act with horror, and would never dare to destroy the earthly tabernacle given him by God. In these respects, as I have said, we possess rare advantages. It is a great favor from God to have this light. There is no unwillingness on His part to communicate it; but there is an unwillingness on the part of the children of men to receive it when it is communicated.[8]

Along this same line of thought, but in more recent times, President Harold B. Lee has expressed his view that a person can best maintain and even restore his self-respect if he or she fully understands the answer to "Who am I?" and "From where did I come?" A portion of President Lee's statement is given below:

> "Who am I?" Those lacking in that important understanding, and, consequently, in some degree those failing to hold themselves in the high esteem which they would have if they did understand, are lacking self-respect....
> A great psychologist, MacDougall, once said; "The first thing to be done to help a man to moral regeneration is to restore, if possible, his self-respect." Also I recall the prayer of the old English weaver, "O God, help me to hold a high opinion of myself." That should be the prayer of every soul;

not an abnormally developed self-esteem that becomes haughtiness, conceit, or arrogance, but a righteous self-respect that might be defined as "belief in one's own worth, worth to God, and worth to man."

Now consider these answers to the searching questions which must be burned into the consciousness of all those who have strayed away or who have not arrived at a true evaluation of themselves in this world of chaos.... May I ask each of you again the question, "Who are you?" You are all the sons and daughters of God. Your spirits were created and lived as organized intelligences before the world was. You have been blessed to have a physical body because of your obedience to certain commandments in that premortal state. You are now born into a family to which you have come, into the nations through which you have come, as a reward for the kind of lives you lived before you came here and at a time in the world's history...determined by the faithfulness of each of those who lived before this world was created....

All these rewards were seemingly promised, or fore-ordained, before the world was. Surely these matters must have been determined by the kinds of lives we had lived in that premortal spirit world. Some may question these assumptions, but at the same time they will accept without any question the belief that each one of us will be judged when we leave this earth according to his or her deeds during our lives here in mortality. Isn't it just as reasonable to believe that what we have received here in this earth life was given to each of us according to the merits of our conduct before we came here?...

If we can get a person to think what those words mean, then we can begin to understand the significance of the words of the renowned psychologist, MacDougall, from whom I have previously quoted, "The first thing to be done to help a man to moral regeneration is to restore, if possible, his self-respect." How better may that self-respect be restored than to help him to fully understand the answer to that question, "Who am I?"...

I would charge you to say again and again to yourselves, as the Primary organization has taught the children to sing, "I am a (son or a daughter) of God" and by so doing, begin today to live closer to those ideals which will make your life happier and more fruitful because of an awakened realization of who you are.[9.]

It is with the intent of answering as fully as possible the questions "Who am I?" and "Where did I come from?" that this book has been written. It is the author's hope that those who read this book will seek inspiration from the Holy Ghost as to the truthfulness of the information contained herein and apply that knowledge in such a way that righteousness will always prevail in their lives.

CHAPTER TWO

The Eternal Elements of Pre-Mortality

The Entity of Intelligence or Spirit Element

In our pre-mortal life each person who has lived, does live, or will live on this earth first existed as "intelligence" or "spirit element" and then secondly as "organized intelligences" or "spirit children" of our Father in heaven. [1]

Joseph Smith, the prophet of the restoration of the gospel in this dispensation, taught that our first existence in pre-mortality was as an "intelligence" or "spirit element," and that this "intelligence" or "spirit element" was an "individual entity" of substance which had "no beginning" nor end and which could be rightfully termed the "ego" or "mind" of man. In essence, the Prophet stated that our pre-mortal "intelligence" is today that part of our being with which we do our thinking.[2] For example, he once said:

> The mind or the intelligence which man possesses is co-equal (co-eternal) with God Himself.... I am dwelling on the immortality of the spirit of man. It is logical to say that the intelligence of spirits is immortal and yet that it had a beginning? The intelligence of spirits had no beginning, neither will it have an end. That is good logic. That which has a beginning may have an end. There never was a time when there were not spirits; for they are co-equal (co-eternal) with our Father in heaven.... Intelligence is eternal and exists upon a self-existent principle. It is a spirit from age to age, and there is no creation about it.[3]

As to the specific nature of the entity of "intelligence" or "spirit element," the Lord has revealed that "intelligence" is the "light of truth" and is a self-existent substance[4] which, like "spirit matter," is more "fine or pure" than what mortal man can now detect or understand. This is given to us in the D & C, sections 93 and 131:

> Man was also in the beginning with God. Intelligence, or the light of truth, was not created or made, neither indeed can be.
>
> All truth is independent in that sphere in which God has placed it, to act for itself, as all intelligence also; otherwise there is no existence . . . .
>
> For man is spirit. The elements are eternal, and spirit and element, inseparably connected, receive a fulness of joy;
>
> And when separated, man cannot receive a fulness of joy . . . .
>
> There is no such thing as immaterial matter. All spirit is matter, but it is more fine or pure, and can only be discerned by purer eyes;
>
> We cannot see it; but when our bodies are purified we shall see that it is all matter.[5]

Similarly, the Prophet Joseph Smith taught that the terms "element" and "matter" were synonymous, which suggests that "spirit element" or "intelligence" is a kind of "refined matter:"[6]

> Hence we infer that God had materials to organize the world out of chaos—chaotic matter, which is element, and in which dwells all the glory. Element had an existence from the time he had.[7]

Also, the Prophet has additionally stated that "the intelligence of spirits is immortal," having no beginning or end, and that "the pure principles of element . . . may be organized and re-organized, but not destroyed."[8] This again suggests that "spirit element" or "intelligence" is a kind of "matter," for modern science knows today that matter can likewise be changed or re-organized into energy, or vice versa, but may not be either created or destroyed.[9]

President Joseph Fielding Smith once said that it may be "futile" for Latter-day Saints to endeavor to explain exactly what an intelligence is since "we have never been given any insight into this matter beyond what the Lord has fragmentarily revealed."[10] Nevertheless, some Latter-day Saint scientists have tried from time to time to explain the specific nature and composition of "intelligence." For example, in 1845 Elder Orson Pratt, an apostle, wrote the following:

> What is intelligence?—It must be either a property of material atoms, or a result of the combination or contact of those atoms.
>
> If intelligence be a property of material atoms prior to their combination or contact with other atoms, then it is evident that this property could not have been derived by experience from external things. It is still further evident, that this intelligent property could not have been derived from any internal operations, for such operations would be impossible in a perfectly solid and imporus atom. Hence, it could not have been derived from any source, either external or internal. Therefore, if intelligence be a property of material atoms, it must have been as eternal as the substance to which it belongs.
>
> Perhaps, some may argue, that material atoms receive intelligence not by coming into contact or union with external things, but by the will of some intelligent atom or being. But how could an intelligent being impart this property to matter without acting upon it, by bringing something external into contact with it? It would be as impossible as it would be to act upon nothing and produce something. But to say that some being gave this property to atoms is to admit the prior existence of a being with intelligence. How did this being derive or acquire its intelligence? Was it derived by experience, or was it as eternal as the being itself?—To say it was derived by experience, is to admit that this being was acted upon from without, which is contrary to the above supposition. Therefore its intelligence, if not derived from experience, must have been eternal. And if the intelligence of one atom or being has been external, anology would say that the intelligence of all other atoms or beings may have been eternal also. And reason has demonstrated that the intelligence of every atom must either be without a beginning, or else be the recall of contact and combination.[11]

More recently, Elder W. Cleon Skousen, professor of ancient scripture at Brigham Young University, has expressed a more detailed theory of what "intelligence or spirit element" may be:

> Already the Lord has revealed far more than the members of the Church have been able to digest. In fact, it is

apparent from a review of the writings of Joseph Smith, Brigham Young, Heber C. Kimball, Orson Pratt and other early leaders of the Church, that they enjoyed a far deeper insight into these revelations than the body of the Church today. Our task in this generation is not to plead for more revelations on the secrets of the universe, but to digest what we already have in preparation for those yet to come.

Science, meanwhile, has caught up with some of the early revelations to the Church, and demonstrated in a tangible way those things which the Saints were formerly required to accept on faith. Some of these we shall be discussing later. Undoubtedly, L.D.S. scientists could have been pioneers in a greater number of fields if they had taken the Lord at His word and set up research teams to probe the cosmic secrets of life and nature in those dimensions where the Lord had revealed that truth could be found. Too often, these great discoveries had to wait on the tedious trial-and-error methods of worldly scholars to disclose what L.D.S. scientists should have known all along....

The human mind cannot conceive of anything which "always existed," yet the Lord assures us that the family of Gods themselves and everything they have organized to fill up their cosmic space with organized kingdoms are merely manifestations and combinations of two eternal ingredients—*intelligences and elements.*

Both of these exist in limitless quantities in the eternities and the work and glory of the superior intelligences whom we honor as Gods or Supreme Beings consist in organizing, educating, testing and elevating these eternal intelligences in embodiments of highly refined matter until they attain the power and glory of Godhood or some lesser level for which they are qualified.

We have no idea what the form or nature of a primitive intelligence might be like, the Lord has never revealed it. But we know a lot about the *qualities* of an intelligence simply because that is what each of us are. We observe certain things about ourselves which are marvelous to contemplate.

First of all, we are self-knowing. With the famous French philosopher and mathematician, Rene Descartes (1596-1650), we can say, *"Cogito ergo sum"*—I think, therefore, I am. As God said of Himself, "I am that I am," meaning He is a self-existing, eternal being (Exodus 3:14). The same is also true of us, but we wouldn't have known we were eternal had not the Lord revealed it, because our memory of the past has been completely tuned out. God assures us that we were "in the beginning with God." Then He goes on to say that we each existed as an intelligence which was "NOT created, neither indeed can be." (D & C 93:29)

Therefore, we ALWAYS existed out there in the eternities. This fact we must accept on faith without being able to rationally comprehend it because it defies human understanding. Nevertheless, the Lord assured Abraham that intelligences "have no beginning, they existed before, they shall have no end, they shall exist after, for they are gnolaum, or eternal." (Abraham 3:18)

An intelligence, then, was not created and it cannot be destroyed. But it can be magnified....

In a sense, the enlargement of an intelligence is an awakening process. It is one of self-realization. This marvelous phenomenon is possible because the intelligence has certain inherent qualities. It not only knows it exists, but it can observe, remember, associate previous observations and experiences, imagine, idealize, think creatively, design creatively, and most remarkably of all, express a wholly independent discrimination by manifesting a will to act or not to act. The Lord assures us that this is a correct evaluation. He says every existing thing is "independent in that sphere in which God has placed it, to act for itself, as all intelligence also; otherwise there is no existence"—meaning no existence in God's organized kingdoms. (D & C 93:30) Whatever can be observed in God's vast creations is there because it voluntarily wishes to be there and doing what it is doing. Apparently the Gods learned long ago that any degree of compulsion or violation of free agency introduces into the system the seeds of civil war, revolution and cosmic dissolution. Therefore the first rule of heaven is achieving all that is achieved by voluntary participation. That is why the scripture says that when vast concourses of intelligences are commanded to do something, the Gods "watched those things which they had ordered until they obeyed." (Abraham 4:18) The Gods accomplish everything through a voluntary system of obedience, not a mechanical or automatic compliance based on force and compulsion. This precept is fundamental to an understanding of how God and His priesthood function in the universe.

The Lord has revealed to His prophets that an intelligence by itself is extremely limited. To advance it has to be associated with a quantity of matter or "element," (as the Lord calls it). It is through organizations of matter that the intelligences are able to achieve embodiments for self-expression, emotional satisfaction, and tabernacled glory. As Joseph Smith declared, "Element is eternal. In it dwells all the glory." (*Teachings of Joseph Smith*, p. 96) Or, as Brigham Young described it, "...qualities and attributes depend entirely upon their connection with organized matter for their development and visible manifestation." (*Journal of Discourses*, Vol. 11:121)

The Lord verifies this fact, saying, "The elements are eternal, and *spirit* [a refined form of matter] and *element* [belonging to the earth] inseparably connected [in the resurrection] receive a fulness of joy. And when separated, man cannot receive a fulness of joy." (D & C 93:33-34)

This demonstrates that the process of uniting intelligences with embodiments of matter and elevating them to their fullest potential of glory is an elaborately complex procedure. And we are right in the midst of ours. Here is the way we are told that we arrived at our present state.

First of all, we were tested as intelligences. No details are revealed concerning this, but it must have been over a tremendous period of time. Finally we were ready to be "locked-in" with organizations of element and that is what God calls "the beginning." It appears that the majority of intelligences were locked in with single particles of matter which in turn were organized and compounded together to form little universes, called atoms; they, in turn, into molecules; molecules into complex orders of substances to form suns, planets and moons.

All of this "organizing" was made possible by attaching intelligences to particles of matter. As Brigham Young said, "Matter is capacitated to receive intelligence." (*Journal of Discourses,* Vol. 7, p. 2)

We now know the intelligences were assigned to embodiments of matter on various levels according to their capacity. During the original testing of the intelligences by the Gods, there must have been a severe grading system to determine the level on which they would be assigned. Joseph Smith recorded that on March 1, 1842, he instructed the Quorum of the Twelve and their wives on "many important principles in relation to progressive improvement in the scale of intelligent existence." (*Doc. Hist. of the Church,* Vol. 4, p. 519) Abraham also recorded a revelation in which the Lord described how the intelligences were "organized" on their various levels and how the intelligence on one level was superceded by those on the next level until they reached the highest intelligence of all, which is God. (Abraham 3:17-19)

We have already mentioned the intelligences which were locked in on the 1) planetary level. A higher order was locked in on the level of 2) plant life, the next on the level of 3) animal life, and the highest intelligences were given charge of marvelous embodiments fashioned in the 4) image of God and actually begotten of Him. We are they....

Now that we have seen how extensive the Lord has used organized intelligences in "all things" to control matter, we need to examine some of the inherent qualities of an intelligence which will help us to understand how God has organized them. The most profound implications are contained in one of the modern revelations which says: "The glory of God is intelligence, or, in other words, *light and truth.*" (D & C 93:36)

This would suggest that if we want to have a better understanding of "intelligence," we should try to get a better understanding of "light" and "truth." This turns out to be a very profitable line of research.

By making intelligence synonymous with "light" the Lord seems to be telling us that intelligence is constantly radiating a manifestation of what it is and what it is doing. In a sense it is constantly broadcasting light and knowledge of itself. And knowledge is what "truth" is. The Lord describes truth as "*knowledge* of things as they are, as they were, and as they are to come." (D & C 93:24) This capacity of intelligence to constantly broadcast or illuminate other intelligences with a knowledge of what it is, constitutes the light of reality or the "light of truth" spoken of in the Doctrine and Covenants (88:6). If we think of "truth" as everything as it really is, then we can think of intelligence as broadcasting or radiating what it "really is."

And the Lord assures us that this is exactly what happens. He tells us that "truth shineth" (D & C 88:7), or radiates to other intelligences a knowledge of what it is, what it has been, and what it will be.

God, as the super-intelligence of our order, also radiates a knowledge of His being, His will, and His work. Therefore His truth "shineth," and because it is so brilliant and all pervasive it is identified as *the* light which "proceedeth forth from the presence of God to fill the immensity of space." (D & C 88:12) The Savior is the medium through which it is diffused to our part of the universe; so it is sometimes called the "light of Christ." (D & C 88:7)

Now the Lord tells us something very interesting about this radiation process among the intelligences. He says these obedient intelligences in alliance with the Father will not share their message with the adversary: "light and truth forsake that evil one." (D & C 93:37) In fact, the Lord says it is the purpose of the adversary to get intelligent beings to be disobedient to God so that other intelligences will no longer communicate with them and thus he "taketh away light and truth, through disobedience, from the children of men." (D & C 98:39) The absence of light and a knowledge of what is going on (truth) therefore leaves rebellious personalities in a state of "darkness" and if it continues, it becomes a state of absolute alienation and total isolation from the entire communications system of God's organized cosmos. Such creatures gradually find themselves slipping away into a terrible abyss of quarrantined detention called *"outer darkness,"* where they are insulated away from both light and knowledge. Therefore it is a place of "weeping, and wailing, and gnashing of teeth." (D & C 101:91)

On the other hand, when an intelligent being seeks to struggle and progress and obey God's commandments, he "receiveth truth and light until he is glorified and *knoweth all things.*" (D & C 93:28) This simply means that if a person can increase and refine his powers of perception through righteousness until he eliminates all darkness from himself and receives every radiation of light from everything that exists, then he can truly be in a position to know and comprehend all things just as God does. This is a specific promise made to God's valiant Saints following their resurrection. (D & C 93:26 plus 88:107)

And if we are able to receive a communication from "all things" it is easy to comprehend how it would be possible to anticipate prophetically what is going to happen in the future. This is why God is able to know "all things from the beginning." (1 Nephi 9:6) It is on this basis that God can reveal the future to His prophets and tell exactly what will happen unless some additional factor is thrown into the great eternal computer. Thus He warns each generation of pending calamities so that they can repent and change the course of coming events, for He can already see what is coming if they do not.[12]

In concluding this sub-chapter on "The Entity of Intelligence," the author would like all Latter-day Saints to remember the following caution which has been given by the Church about the proper understanding and correct meaning of the term "intelligence:"

It should be remembered that the reference to "intelligences" is to an identity we each have composed of our spirit and that part of our eternal nature presently referred to as "intelligence." It is not intended to convey the impression that status in his kingdom or in the Church is based on intellectual capacity, a phrase often equated with intelligence. Many other qualities and virtues, love, faith, humility, patience, kindness, self-effacement, etc. are as significant in terms of our relationships with God and with others as is intellectual capacity. The term "superior" used in reference to those called to positions of leadership must be construed to mean that they are better qualified to lead, but not necessarily that they are "superior" in terms of spirituality or moral qualities.[13]

The Entity of Organized Intelligences or Spirit Children

Following our existence in pre-mortality as an "intelligence" or "spirit element," we eventually progressed until we became "organized intelligences" or "spirit children" of our Father in heaven. Concerning this new state of our pre-earthly existence, Elder Daniel Ludlow has written:

The scriptures are not too clear on the exact status of the intelligence before it became an "organized intelligence" or in other words before it was clothed with a spiritual body by God. However, the scriptures are definite that we all became organized intelligences (see Abraham 3:22), and from this time forth we rightfully began to refer to God as our Father. This was our spiritual birth, and through it we all became sons and daughters unto God. Thus, we are all truly brothers and sisters, for we are spiritually all sons and daughters of God.[14]

As "organized intelligences" or "spirit children" of our Father in Heaven, we became an entity of "spirit" possessing a "spiritual body" which was more pure and refined but yet similar in form to the mortal bodies we now possess.[15] In this birth as the spirit children of our Heavenly Father (and our *Heavenly Mother*), our previous "intelligence or spirit element" was organized through a literal but spiritual birth process into embodied spiritual entities[16] which then acquired definite form, "size, shape and function."[17] As Elder William Berrett has said, our pre-mortal "spiritual bodies" possessed:

> ...bodies of spirit, in form like unto the present man, definite in size, shape and function. (see Ether 3:14-16.) They could converse with one another (see Moses 4:1-2; Abraham 3:27), exercise their free will in the matter of choices (see Moses 4:3-4), experience anger (Abraham 3:28), and have joy (see Job 38:49). In short, except for certain limitations, which lack of a physical body entails, and the limitation of environment, they must have enjoyed the association of one another and listened to the teachings of one another, like unto man as we know him on this earth.[18]

In Chapter Four of this book we will review more fully our pre-mortal spiritual birth and relationship to our Heavenly Father (and our Heavenly Mother). However, we should remember that in our pre-mortal existence our "intelligence" or "spirit element" was eventually organized through a spiritual birth process into an "organized intelligence" which so far as scripture records, is likewise called a "spirit, soul, or spirit child" of our Father in heaven.[19]

Similarities and Relationships of Matter, Intelligence, and Spirit

The similarities and relationships of matter, intelligence, and spirit to each and one another is not as perplexing as it may seem. Elder James E. Talmage, a respected Latter-day Saint scientist and theologian, expressed in the early part of this century his understanding that matter, intelligence, and spirit only "differed in degree rather than in kind."[20] The following statement is that of Elder Talmage. Although it is brief, it is clear, concise, and remarkably comprehensive in covering the topic stated above:

> Science and scripture testify to the fact that matter is indestructible, and of necessity uncreated in the inconsistent sense of having been brought into existence from nothing. Creation means organization and association, whereby matter may be made to assume unlimited variations as to constitution and form, and to serve an infinitude of application and purpose.
>
> It is through matter that spirit, regarded as the life-force itself, operates and functions. We are accustomed to think of spirit and matter as distinct entities; and this conception is measurably correct if we remember that spirit, far from being substanceless, differs from matter rather in degree than in kind.
>
> "There is no such thing as immaterial matter. All spirit is matter, but it is more fine or pure, and can only be discerned by purer eyes." (Doctrine & Covenants 131:7.)
>
> Supporting this inspired utterance, we have abundant analogies in nature. Take for example hydrogen, which is a colorless, odorless, tasteless gas, therefore not perceptible through the unaided senses, and so tenuous that only tight vessels can hold it confined. Nevertheless, by highly developed methods we have learned to weigh it, measure it in bulk, and otherwise manipulate it. Moreover, we know how to create it, in the sense of isolating it from other elements with which it had been previously combined. But even the tyro in chemistry, as well as every intelligent thinker, knows that such isolation is not a creation in the long accepted but wholly untrue sense of making the gas out of nothing.
>
> Aside from its distinguishing chemical properties, hydrogen differs essentially from other elements through its lightness or low specific gravity. And so the tenuous substance we call spirit differs greatly from the grosser stuff we call matter, in density, and doubtless in other properties unknown to us.
>
> As the material elements combine into definite compounds, or become organized into tissue, plant, animal, or human, and so appear, for example, as an embodied tree, dog, or man, according to the grade of vital force acting upon them, so may spirit be organized by the operation of superior forces into living beings. Such spirit-creatures, though as

yet temporally unembodied individuals, the Lord has designated by the expressive term intelligences. A Divine revelation recorded by Abraham amply illustrates this condition:

"Now the Lord had shown unto me, Abraham, the intelligences that were organized before the world was; and among all these there were many of the noble and great ones. And God saw these souls that they were good...and He said unto me: Abraham, thou art one of them; thou wast chosen before thou wast born." (Pearl of Great Price, p. 66)....

God the Eternal Father is the Parent of the spirits of mankind. He created them from eternally existent matter as organized intelligences. We are the children of eternal parentage; and as God is eternal, so are we, for to our existence there will be, can be, no end.[21]

CHAPTER THREE

The Nature of God In Pre-Mortality

The Order of the Gods

As Latter-day Saints, we recognize that there are three glorified, exalted, and perfected personages who comprise the Godhead—the Supreme Presidency of our universe. They are God the Father (Elohim), God the Son (Jehovah, or Jesus Christ), and God the Holy Ghost. God the Father and God the Son possess glorified bodies of flesh and bones, while God the Holy Ghost is a personage of Spirit. Speaking in the proper finite sense, these three are the only Gods we worship.[1]

In addition to our Godhead, however, there is an infinite number of Holy Personages drawn from worlds without number who have also passed on to exaltation and are thus Gods.[2] From the scriptures and through the discourses of the Prophet Joseph Smith and other general authorities of the Church, we learn that our own Father in Heaven "had a Father," who likewise "had a Father,"...and so on...back through the eternal eons of time.[3] In reference to this concept of our Father in Heaven having a Father...and thus there being an eternal succession of Gods, Elder Bruce R. McConkie, quoting the Prophet Joseph Smith, has written the following:

> Paul taught, "There be gods many, and lords many," adding that "to us there is but one God, the Father, of whom are all things, and we in him; and one Lord Jesus Christ, by whom are all things, and we by him. Howbeit there is not in every man that knowledge." (1 Cor. 8:4-7; D & C 121:28-32.) The Prophet commenting on this passage said: "Paul had no

allusion to the heathen gods. I have it from God, and get over it if you can. I have a witness of the Holy Ghost, and a testimony that Paul had no allusion to the heathen gods in the text." (*Teachings,* p. 371.)

The Prophet also taught—in explaining John's statement, "And hath made us kings and priests unto *God and his Father"* (Rev. 1:6)—that there is "a god above the Father of our Lord Jesus Christ.... *If Jesus Christ was the Son of God, and John discovered that God the Father of Jesus Christ had a Father, you may suppose that he had a Father also.* Where was there ever a son without a father? And where was there ever a father without first being a son? Whenever did a tree or anything spring into existence without a progenitor? And everything comes in this way. Paul says that which is earthly is in the likeness of that which is heavenly. Hence if Jesus had a Father, can we not believe that *he* had a Father also?" (*Teachings,* pp. 370-373.)

Indeed, this doctrine of plurality of Gods is so comprehensive and glorious that it reaches out and embraces every exalted personage. Those who attain exaltation are gods. "Go and read the vision in the Book of Covenants," the Prophet said. "There is clearly illustrated glory upon glory— one glory of the sun, another glory of the moon, and a glory of the stars; and as one star differeth from another star in glory, even so do they of the telestial world differ in glory, and *every man who reigns in celestial glory is a God to his dominions.... They who obtain a glorious resurrection from the dead are exalted far above principalities, powers, thrones, dominions, and angels, and are expressly declared to be heirs of God and joint-heirs with Jesus Christ, all having eternal power."* (*Teachings,* p. 374.) [4]

As is obvious from the preceding statements of the Prophet Joseph Smith, as summarized by Elder McConkie, there is indeed an order of succession in the genealogy and family of the Eternal Gods of heaven. However, this order of succession is just not limited to genealogy, but rather encompasses all that the Eternal Gods strive to accomplish, for all the Eternal Gods perpetuate the same eternal truths and accomplishments that have gone before them. For example, during the period of our pre-mortal existence when we resided as "intelligences" or "spirit element," "the family of the Gods" was busy enlarging their creations to accommodate our future presence, first as actual entities of spirit, then as mortal beings, and then as eventual resurrected personages.[5] Concerning this subject, Elder Cleon Skousen has written the following:

> As we shall see in a moment, the Lord has revealed that the infinite regions of eternity are filled with vast concourses of unorganized intelligences and chaotic bits of unorganized matter. These were never created, nor can they be destroyed. They are eternal realities. However, they can be organized, reorganized and disorganized.
>
> In order to organize them, it was necessary for the superior intelligences—the family of the Gods—to sweep clean certain areas of eternity and commence the building of organized kingdoms. How and when this was done we are not told, but we are assured that this conquered territory or "space" which belongs to the Gods is now completely subordinate to the will of the Gods. The Lord says "...there is *no* space in the which there is no kingdom...either a greater or a lesser kingdom. And unto every kingdom is given a law, and unto every law there are certain bounds also and conditions." (D & C 88:37-38.)
>
> This would clearly signify that unorganized intelligences and chaotic bits of matter which do not yet belong to God's order are kept outside this region. Therefore the "space" God is talking about is finite and has boundaries. No doubt this "space" is being constantly expanding as the family of Gods scoop up additional quantities of unorganized "material" to build new kingdoms and therefore push back the boundaries of "space" to accommodate the latest additions.
>
> This conclusion is in harmony with the Lord's declaration that His course is "one eternal round" (1 Nephi 10:19; D & C 3:2; 35:1). This would suggest that what was done in the past to organize kingdoms is being repeated by the Gods. Therefore, the process of conquering additional territory and pushing back the unorganized forces in outer darkness would have to be a continuing operation whereby the "space" belonging to the family of the Gods would be constantly expanding.
>
> Grasping the implications of these revelations helps us to appreciate what an extraordinary and wonderful blessing it was to have been fortunate enough to be scooped up from the chaos of outer darkness and thereupon given a chance to qualify for some part in the organized dominions of the Gods.

We came in as naked, sleepy, undeveloped intelligences and we are where we are today because we exerted ourselves and responded with zeal and eagerness to the opportunities given us. All of those primitive beginnings were aeons ago and since then we have travelled a course of perilous adventure, rigorous testing, stringent competition, and threatened elimination, until today we have arrived on the very threshold of godhood.[6]

The Prophet Joseph Smith stated that as a God our own Father in Heaven instituted laws in the beginning "whereby the rest" of the numerous intelligences within His infinite regions of eternity "could have a privilege to advance like himself:"

The first principles of man are self-existent with God. God himself, finding he was in the midst of spirits and glory, because he was more intelligent, saw proper to institute laws whereby the rest could have a privilege to advance like himself. The relationship we have with God places us in a situation to advance in knowledge. He has power to institute laws to instruct the weaker intelligences, that they may be exalted with himself, so that they might have one glory upon another, and all that knowledge, power, glory, and intelligence, which is requisite in order to save them in the world of spirits....[7]

The Progression of God Our Father

The Prophet Joseph Smith once said that our Father in Heaven "was once as we are now" and "dwelt upon an earth," but that He is presently "an exalted man...or a God."[8] As Latter-day Saints we also realize that we can eventually progress to the stature of a God if we will but exercise full diligence and obedience to the principles and ordinances of the gospel in this life and the next. In 1876 Elder Orson Pratt said the following in regard to the progression of our Father in Heaven being similar to our own:

A great many have supposed that God the Eternal Father, whom we worship in connection with his Son, Jesus Christ, was always a self-existing, eternal being from all eternity, that he had no beginning as a personage. But in order to illustrate this, let us inquire, What is our destiny? If we are now the sons and daughters of God, what will be our future destiny?... Will we ever become Gods?...

By living according to every word which proceeds from the mouth of God, we shall attain to his likeness, the same as our children grow up and become like their parents; and, as children through diligence attain to the wisdom and knowledge of their parents, so may we attain to the knowledge of our Heavenly Parents, and if they be obedient to this commandment, they will not only be called the sons of God, but be gods....

Says one, to carry it out still further, "if we become gods and are glorified like unto him, our bodies fashioned like unto his most glorious body, may not he have passed through a mortal ordeal as we mortals are now doing? Why not? If it is necessary for us to obtain experience through the things that are presented before us in this life, why not those beings, who are already exalted and become gods, obtain their experience in the same way? We would find, were we to carry this subject from world to world, from our world to another, even to the endless ages of eternity, that there never was a time but what there was a Father and Son. In other words, when you entertain that which is endless, you exclude the idea of a first being, a first world; the moment you admit of a first, you limit the idea of endless. The chain itself is endless, but each link had its beginning.

Says one, "This is incomprehensible." It may be so in some respects. We can admit, though, that duration is endless, for it is impossible for man to conceive of a limit to it. If duration is endless, there can never be a first minute, a first hour, or first period; endless duration in the past is made up of a continuation of endless successive moments—it had no beginning. Precisely so with regard to this endless succession of personages; there never will be a time when fathers, and sons, and worlds will not exist; neither was there ever a period through all the past ages of duration, but what there was a world, and a Father and Son, a redemption and exaltation to the fullness and power of the Godhead.[9]

In reflection, Latter-day Saints should remember, however, that although our Father in Heaven once progressed upon a path similar to our own—from pre-mortality—to mortality—to immortality, nevertheless, He is not progressing now "in knowledge, truth, virtue, wisdom, or any of the attributes of godliness. He has already gained these things in their fullness. He is only progressing in the sense that His creations increase, His dominions expand, His spirit offspring multiply, and more kingdoms are added to His domains."[10]

The Greatness of Our Father in Heaven

The gospel teaches us that God our Eternal Father is all-powerful, all knowing, and all good. He is the Creater, Ruler, and Preserver of all things, and His total greatness and majesty is incomprehensible to mortal man. In speaking of some of the majestic attributes and characteristics which our Father in Heaven possesses, the Prophet Joseph Smith has said:

> That God is the only supreme governor and independent Being in whom all fulness and perfection dwell; who is omnipotent, omnipresent, and omniscient; without beginning of days or end of life; and that in him every good gift and every good principle dwell; and that he is the Father of lights; in him the principle of faith dwells independently, and he is the object in whom the faith of all other rational and accountable beings centers for life and salvation. (*Lectures on Faith,* p. 9.)
>
> There is a God in heaven, who is infinite and eternal, from everlasting to everlasting the same unchangeable God, the framer of heaven and earth, and all things which are in them.[11]

And Elder Orson Pratt has likewise expressed:

> It is declared, as part of the belief of the Methodists, that God is without passions. Love is one of the great passions of God. Love is everywhere declared a passion, one of the noblest passions of the human heart. This principle of love is one of the attributes of God. "God is love," says the Apostle John," and he that dwelleth in love dwelleth in God, and God in him." If, then, this is one of the great attributes of Jehovah, if he is filled with love and compassion towards the children of men, if his son Jesus Christ so loved the world that he gave his life to redeem mankind from the effects of the fall, then, certainly, God the Eternal Father must be in possession of this passion. Again, he possesses the attribute of Justice, which is sometimes called Anger, but

the real name of this attribute is Justice. "He executeth justice," says the Psalmist; also, "Justice and judgment are the habitation of thy throne." Justice is one of the noble characteristics of our heavenly Father; hence another of his passions.[12]

In regard to the "glory" of our Father in Heaven, Elder Hyrum L. Andrus, professor of Church History and Doctrine at Brigham Young University, has observed that "the glory of God...is, in its basic and fundamental elements, a concentration of celestial light and truth or celestial intelligence to a point of brilliance above the brightness of the sun:"

"The glory of God is intelligence, or, in other words, light and truth." (D & C 93:36.)
Sometimes we use this statement loosely when we talk about the glory of God. It means, to most of us, that God takes glory in being intelligent. I am sure that He does. But the fuller meaning of this particular statement is this: that which constitutes the everlasting burnings in which God dwells, that which constitutes this brilliance of light which would cause the sun to hide its face in shame is God's glory. It is, in its basic and fundamental elements, a concentration of celestial light and truth or celestial intelligence to a point of brilliance above the brightness of the sun. Imagine if you can a being in whose image you were created, a being who has centered within himself such an intense concentration of pure intelligence and its correlated attributes and powers, that the very brilliance of that person would outshine the sun in the firmament. When you can comprehend that glorified person's intellect, so that you see as He sees, understand as He understands, feel as He feels, then you can begin to say that you know God. When you can meet him on an intellectual level, when you can comprehend as he comprehends, then you will know God—not until then. That is not likely to happen in this mortal state. Moses was allowed to see the glory of God in some measure, not in full—it is not possible for man in mortality to behold the fulness of this light and glory—and when Moses went away from that experience, he gave us this statement, "Now, for this cause I know that man is nothing, which thing I never had supposed." (Moses 1:10.) Sometimes we do not think about the great disparity that exists between man and God.

We take pleasure in proving to the world that God is an anthropomorphic being, that He is a being in likeness and form much like man. After we have satisfied ourselves with the fact that we have won the argument, then we cease to think about God and do not consider the divine injunction that it is life eternal to know Him. It is almost an eternal process to acquire the intelligence by which we can know Him.

This is the key that I would like to give you concerning the nature and majesty of God. God is a being of glory, and the glory associated with Him is essentially a concentration of all the forces of life, of intelligence, of truth, and of light in the universe. Such a concentration of power and of truth within Him makes Him a being in brightness of the sun. [13]

Concerning the power which our omnipotent Father in Heaven exercises, in and over all things throughout His universe, Elder Cleon Skousen has written that God our Father "has revealed...that His personal power is the result of the 'honor' which is accorded Him by the intelligences of the universe;" and that God has had to "earn" this power just as we will if we even intend to become like Him. The following is Elder Skousen's discourse:

Anyone who has received instruction in the holy temples of God has learned the basic lesson that the universe is under the direction of God through numerous levels of delegated authority. This authority to act in the name of God and carry out God's purposes is called "Priesthood." The word "priest" has its derivation from "presbyter" or Elder which literally means "leader of the flock." The word, "Priest-hood" means all of those, collectively, who enjoy the calling of Elders or leaders of the flock of God.

Of course, the most remarkable and impressive thing about God's handiwork is the *order* which exists at all levels. This "order" is maintained by having all of the descending ranks of officers in the various kingdoms of God strictly obey the pattern given them. Emerson thought the first law of heaven was order, but *modern revelation has disclosed that the first law of heaven is obedience.* (D & C 130:20-21.) Order is the result.

Even the Priesthood of God has always been known as an "order" because it constitutes the line of delegated authority through which God accomplishes His orderly purposes. Originally, it was called the "order of the Only Begotten Son;" then it became identified with one of God's greatest servants during the pre-flood epic and was called the "order of Enoch." (D & C 76:57.) Enoch created the most peaceful, prosperous, and righteous society in the history of the antediluvian world, so that ultimately his entire order was translated. (*Inspired Version,* Genesis 7:78, plus *Teachings of Joseph Smith*, p. 158) After the flood, another great prophet and ruler succeeded in duplicating on a smaller scale what Enoch had done. His name was Melchizedek. He, too, succeeded in having his entire society translated (*Inspired Version*, Genesis 14:32-34), and thereafter the people identified the true Priesthood of God as the "order of Melchizedek." (D & C 76:57.)

It was in the pre-existence or First Estate that we were trained in Priesthood service. Many were called, but not all were chosen. Those who were valiant, zealous and resourceful in helping the Father get His work done, were "chosen" and foreordained during the pre-existence to have the privilege of receiving the Priesthood during earth-life. In other words, being in the right place under the right circumstances to receive an investiture of divine authority in this life is no accident. It was earned in the pre-existence. This doctrine is clearly set forth by Alma and Paul.

Alma says those who receive the Priesthood in this life were "called and prepared from the foundation of the world according to the foreknowledge of God." (Alma 13:3) He said this great blessing comes to a man because of his "faith and good works" in the ancient past when God had a foreknowledge of his good works (Alma 13:3).

Paul was another who emphasized that he and his associates had been ordained to their "holy calling" for reasons other than their good works in this life. He said their "holy calling" had all been worked out according to God's purposes and given to them *before* the world began. Here are his exact words:

"Be not thou therefore ashamed of the testimony of our Lord...who hath saved us, and *called* us with an *holy calling,* not according to our *works* but according to his own purposes and grace, which was *given us* in Christ Jesus *before the world began.*" (2 Timothy 1:8-9)

Sometimes we tend to think of Priesthood as merely the order of God in governing His Church. But the truth is that Priesthood represents the "power of God in action" throughout the universe. As Brigham Young said, "If anybody wants to know what the Priesthood of the Son of God is, it is the law by which the worlds are, were, and will continue for ever and ever. It is that system which brings worlds into existence and peoples them, gives them their revolutions...." (*Journal of Discourses*, Vol. 5, p. 127)

The Inspired Version of the Book of Genesis also has something profound to say about the power of the Priesthood in dealing with the forces in the universe. It says that the Lord told Enoch "that every one being ordained after this order and calling should have power, by faith, to break mountains, to divide the seas, to dry up waters, to turn them out of their course; to put at defiance the armies of nations, to divide the earth, to break every band, to stand the presence of God; to do all things according to His will, according to His commands, subdue principalities and powers; and this by the will of the Son of God which was from before the foundation of the world." (*Inspired Version*, Genesis 14:30-31)

Members of the Priesthood know when to exercise this power through direction from the Holy Ghost. In fact, the Holy Ghost uses the quorums of the Priesthood on both sides of the veil to carry out the purposes of God. The Son of God is the manager of the Father's kingdoms and the Holy Ghost is the messenger. As Joseph Smith declared, "The Holy Ghost is God's messenger to administer in all those Priesthoods." (*Doc. Hist. of the Church,* Vol. 5, p. 555)

One final secret which the Lord has revealed concerning His Priesthood is the fact that His personal power is the result of the "honor" which is accorded Him by the intelligences of the universe. (D & C 29:36) If they honor and obey Him, the work of these intelligences is an extension of the righteous will or design of God. If they did not honor and respect Him, His work would be curtailed. This is not only true of God, but of every Priesthood bearer in the universe. To the extent that they are honored, respected and obeyed, they have power.

And that "honor" must be earned. It takes a long time to develop a personality who inspires and maintains the confidence of those intelligent beings under his direction. This is what the Lord was talking about in the Doctrine and Covenants 121:36-37 when He said we must understand:

"That the rights of the priesthood are inseparably connected with the power of heaven, and that the powers of heaven cannot be controlled nor handled only upon the principles of righteousness.

"That they may be conferred upon us, it is true; but when we undertake to cover our sins, or to gratify our pride, our vain ambition, or to exercise control or dominion or compulsion upon the souls of the children of men, in any degree of unrighteousness, behold, the heavens withdraw themselves; the Spirit of the Lord is grieved; and when it is withdrawn, Amen to the Priesthood or the authority of that man."[14]

CHAPTER FOUR

God As the Father of Our Spirits

God is the Father of All Our Spirits

In Chapter Two of this book it was pointed out that following our existence in pre-mortality as an "intelligence" or "spirit element" we eventually progressed until we became "organized intelligences" or "spirit children" of our Father in Heaven. Indeed, there should be no doubt in the minds of Latter-day Saints that our Father in Heaven is the literal Father of "all" of our "spirit entities," and that we are, therefore, His "spirit children." Of this truth the scriptures so declare, as do Latter-day prophets and apostles. For example, President Brigham Young stated this truth emphatically in 1857, when he said:

> I want to tell you, each and every one of you, that you are well acquainted with God our heavenly Father, or the great Eloheim. You are all well acquainted with him, for there is not a soul of you but what has lived in his house and dwelt with him year after year; and yet you are seeking to become acquainted with him, when the fact is, you have merely forgotten what you did know. I told you a little last Sabbath about forgetting things.
>
> There is not a person here today but what is a son or a daughter of that Being. In the spirit world their spirits were first begotten and brought forth, and they lived there with their parents for ages before they came here. This, perhaps, is hard for many to believe, but it is the greatest nonsense in the world not to believe it. If you do not believe it, cease to call him "Father;" and when you pray, pray to some other character.[1]

And in 1876 Elder Orson Pratt likewise expressed:

> We are the offspring of the Lord, but the rest of ani-
> mated nature is not; we are just as much the sons and
> daughters of God as the children in this congregation are the
> sons and daughters of their parents. We are begotten by him.
> When? Before we were born in the flesh.[2]

The Literal Nature of Our Spiritual Birth

As "spirit children" of our Father in Heaven, what was the
nature of our "spiritual birth?" Some Latter-day Saints have as-
sumed that because the Prophet Joseph Smith and some earlier
leaders of the Church sometimes said that "God created the
spirits of men," that our Father in Heaven, therefore, "created or
organized" prior "intelligences" through some type of a "mold-
ing process" into "spirits," rather than their being "literally born
spiritually."[3] This, however, is incorrect. For we are spirit children of our Father in Heaven and of a literal Mother in Heaven,
and were "begotten" through a real "spiritual birth process" into
"embodied spirit entities."[4] Concerning the proper interpretation
of the phrase "God created the spirits of men" Elder Brigham H.
Roberts, one of the Church's early Seven Presidents of the Seventy, has written the following:

> I call attention to this distinction that when in our litera-
> ture we say "God created the spirits of men," it is understood
> that they were "begotten." We mean "generation," *not* "crea-
> tion." Intelligences, which are eternal, uncreated, self-exist-
> ing beings, are begotten spirits, and these afterwards be-
> gotten men. When intelligences are "begotten" spirits they
> are of the nature of him who begets them—sons of God, and
> con-substantial with their Father.[5]

In regard to our having a Mother in Heaven as well as a Father
in Heaven, Elder Bruce R. McConkie has written:

> Implicit in the Christian verity that all men are the spirit
> children of an *Eternal Father* is the usually unspoken truth
> that they are also the offspring of an *Eternal Mother*. An
> exalted and glorified Man of Holiness (Moses 6:57) could
> not be a Father unless a Woman of like glory, perfection, and
> holiness was associated with him as a Mother. The begetting

of children makes a man a father and a woman a mother whether we are dealing with man in his mortal or immortal state.

This doctrine that there is a *Mother in Heaven* was affirmed in plainness by the First Presidency of the Church (Joseph F. Smith, John R. Winder, and Anthon H. Lund) when, in speaking of pre-existence and the origin of man, they said that "man, as a spirit, was begotten and born of *heavenly parents,* and reared to maturity in the eternal mansions of the Father," that man is the "offspring of *celestial parentage,"* and that "all men and women are in the similitude of the *universal Father and Mother,* and are literally the sons and daughters of Deity." (*Man: His Origin and Destiny,* pp. 348-355.)

Mortal persons who overcome all things and gain an ultimate exaltation will live eternally in the family unit and have spirit children, thus becoming Eternal Fathers and Eternal Mothers. (D & C 132:19-32.) Indeed, the formal pronouncement of the Church, issued by the First Presidency and the Council of the Twelve, states: "So far as the stages of eternal progression and attainment have been made known through divine revelation, we are to understand that *only resurrected and glorified beings can become parents of spirit offspring."* (*Man: His Origin and Destiny,* p. 129.)[6]

In addition, regarding the fact that as "spirit children" of our Father in Heaven we were begotten rather than created, President Brigham Young has said the following:

Things were first created spiritually; the Father actually begat the spirits, and they were brought forth and lived with him.... [7]

And also:

Our Father in Heaven begat all the spirits that ever were, or ever will be, upon this earth; and they were born spirits in the eternal world. Then the Lord by His power and wisdom organized the mortal tabernacle of man. We were made first spiritual, and afterwards temporal.[8]

And again:

There is no spirit but what was pure and holy when it came here from the celestial world. There is no spirit among the human family that was begotten in hell; none that were begotten by angels, or by any inferior being. They were not produced by any being less than our Father in heaven. He is the Father of our spirits; and if we could know, understand, and do His will, every soul would be prepared to return back into His presence. And when they get there, they would see that they had formerly lived there for ages, that they had previously been acquainted with every nook and corner, with the palaces, walks, and gardens; and they would embrace their Father, and He would embrace them and say, "My son, my daughter, I have you again;" and the child would say, "O my Father, my Father, I am here again"....[9]

Concerning the exact nature of our being begotten "spirit children" of our Heavenly Father and Mother, Elder Orson Pratt has stated that our spirits "were all born...after the same manner that we are here on earth,...of a literal father and a literal mother." In other words we were born through a birth process which brought forth spiritual bodies rather than mortal bodies:

If we were born in heaven before this world was made, the question might arise as to the nature of that birth. Was it by command that the spiritual substance, scattered through space, was miraculously brought together, and organized into a spiritual form, and called a spirit? Is that the way we were born? Is that the way that Jesus, the firstborn of every creature, was brought into existence? Oh no; we were all born there after the same manner that we are here, that is to say, every person that had an existence before he came here had a literal father and a literal mother, a personal father and a personal mother; hence the Apostle Paul, in speaking to the heathen at Ephesus, says, "We are his offspring." Now I look upon every man and woman that have ever come here on this globe, or that ever will come, as having a father and mother in the heavens by whom their spirits were brought into existence. But how long they resided in the heavens before they came here is not revealed.[10]

Our Spirits Are in the Form of Our Mortal Bodies

As pre-mortal spirit children of our Father in Heaven and Heavenly Mother, we were born with spirit bodies which eventually developed definite form, size, shape and function.[11] In fact, today these spirit bodies of our pre-earthly existence are in a "form and likeness similar to" our own mortal bodies. Regarding this similarity between our pre-mortal spirit bodies and our present mortal bodies Elder Orson Pratt has said:

> We, as Latter-day Saints, believe that the spirits that occupy these tabernacles have form and likeness similar to the human tabernacle. Of course there may be deformities existing in connection with the outward tabernacle which do not exist in connection with the spirit that inhabits it. These tabernacles become deformed by accident in various ways, sometimes at birth, but this may not altogether or in any degree deform the spirits that dwell within them, therefore we believe that the spirits which occupy the bodies of the human family are more or less in the resemblance of the tabernacles.[12]

Likewise, Elder Sterling W. Sill, a member of the First Quorum of Seventy, has also stated:

> Now if you will turn to the 77th Section of the Doctrine and Covenants and read it again, you will find in the second verse it suggests what a spirit looks like. In reply to a number of questions, the following inspired answer is given.
> "...that which is spiritual being in the likeness of that which is temporal; and that which is temporal in the likeness of that which is spiritual; the spirit of man in the likeness of his person, as also the spirit of the beast, and every other creature which God has created." (D & C 77:2.)
> Now, think what those words mean. Every full-grown person who lives upon the earth has a physical body which is the counterpart of the spirit which tabernacles that body. In fact, here the truth is given that all living things have their spiritual entities and that the full-grown or full-sized material creations are the exact counterpart of the spiritual, the spirit-being in the likeness of that which is temporal. In other words if we could see our spirit bodies standing by our sides, we would see that they have the same look, are the same size, have the same shape, and have the same identities.[13]

As to the specific nature of our pre-mortal spirit bodies Elder Melvin J. Ballard, an apostle, said in 1922 that our pre-earthly spirit bodies contained a "substance...more refined and pure and glorious than blood" to sustain us during that period of our existence:

What do we mean by endless or eternal increase? We mean that through the righteousness and faithfulness of men and women who keep the commandments of God they will come forth with celestial bodies, fitted and prepared to enter into their great, high and eternal glory in the celestial kingdom of God, and unto them, through their preparation, there will come children, who will be spirit children. I don't think that is very difficult to comprehend and understand. The nature of the offspring is determined by the nature of the substance that flows in the veins of the being. When blood flows in the veins of the being, the offspring will be what blood produces, which is tangible flesh and bone, but when that which flows in the veins is spirit matter, a substance which is more refined and pure and glorious than blood, the offspring of such beings will be spirit children. By that I mean they will be in the image of the parents. They will have a spirit body and have a spark of the eternal or divine that always did exist in them.

Unto such parentage will this glorious privilege come, for it is written in our scriptures that "the glory of God is to bring to pass the immortality and eternal life of man." So, it will be the glory of men and women that will make their glory like unto His. When the power of endless increase shall come to them, and their offspring, growing and multiplying through ages that shall come, they will be in due time, as we have been, provided with an earth like this, wherein they too may obtain earthly bodies and pass through all the experiences through which we have passed, and then we shall hold our relationship to them, the fulness and completeness of which has not been revealed to us, but we shall stand in our relationship to them as God, our Eternal Father, does to us, and thereby is this the most glorious and wonderful privilege that ever will come to any of the sons and daughters of God. [14]

The Limitations of Our Pre-Mortal Spirit Bodies

In regard to the limitations of our pre-mortal spirit bodies Elder Daniel Ludlow has pointed out that our spirit bodies were apparently not bodies of procreation, that is, spiritual bodies evidently could not give birth to children:

Although the spiritual bodies we had before we came to this earth were the prototypes of the physical bodies we now have, and they were capable of remarkable accomplishments (this is the type of body Jesus Christ had when he created this earth!), yet they had certain limitations. Apparently one of these limitations was that they were not bodies of procreation, that is, spiritual bodies evidently could not give birth to children. Without powers of increase, our possibilities of eternal progression were definitely limited.

In order to give us the opportunity of taking upon ourselves bodies of flesh and bones which would also be bodies of procreation, God our Father called a great council in heaven and presented to us a plan whereby we could share with him the powers of both creation and procreation. This council was undoubtedly one of the most significant events in our pre-earthly existence.[15]

General authorities of the Church have expressed similar thoughts to those of Elder Ludlow. However, further information, beyond the above insight, about the limitation of our spirit bodies not being able to procreate is not available.

As Spirit Offspring of Our Father in Heaven We Are Capable of Becoming Like Him

Because we are the offspring of our Father in Heaven and our Heavenly Mother, we are capable of becoming like them. Through our spirit birth to our Heavenly Parents, they "transmitted to us" their "capabilities, power, and faculties...in an undeveloped state," thereby making it possible for us to become like them if we continue to progress and prove ourselves worthy of eternal exaltation. In 1872 President Lorenzo Snow wrote concerning this subject:

We believe that we are the offspring of our Father in heaven, and that we possess in our spiritual organizations the same capabilities, powers and faculties that our Father possesses, although in an infantile state, requiring to pass through a certain course or ordeal by which they will be developed and improved according to the heed we give to the principles we have received.... We are born in the image of God our Father; he begot us like unto himself. There is the nature of Deity in the composition of our spiritual organization; in our spiritual birth our Father transmitted to us the capabilities, powers and faculties which he himself possessed, as much so as the child on its mother's bosom possesses, although in an undeveloped state, the faculties, powers and susceptibilities of its parent.[16]

And Elder Orson Pratt gave the following comment in 1876:

Before the earth was rolled into existence we were his sons and daughters. Those of his children who prove themselves during this probation worthy of exaltation in his presence, will beget other children, and, precisely according to the same principle, they too will become fathers of spirits, as he is the Father of our spirits; and thus the works of God are one eternal round—creation, glorification, and exaltation in the celestial kingdom.[17]

These and other similar statements present evidence that our pre-mortal spirit birth was a glorious introduction toward mortality, which was so complete that it is possible for each and every one of us to become like our Heavenly Parents if we will righteously and diligently do our part during this mortal life and hereafter.

CHAPTER FIVE

Christ As the Firstborn of Our Father In Heaven

Jesus as the First Son of God in the Spirit

As far as mortal man is concerned, everything centers in Jesus Christ. Because of our Savior's obedience and devotion to eternal truth and knowledge, he attained a pinnacle of intelligence which ranked him as a God—God the Son, the Lord Omnipotent—while yet in the pre-mortal existence. As such, he became, under the direction of our Father in Heaven, the Creator of this earth and of other worlds without number. He was also chosen to work out the atonement and put the whole plan of our redemption, salvation, and exaltation in operation.[1]

Because in pre-mortality Jesus Christ was by far the most intelligent of all the intelligences of our Eternal Father, he became the Firstborn Spirit of our Father in Heaven. Of this, our Lord has said: "And now, verily I say unto you, I was in the beginning with the Father, and am the Firstborn." (D & C 93:21; Col. 1:15) As Latter-day Saints we refer to the Savior as our Elder Brother because of his being the Firstborn of our Father in Heaven. This fact is made clear in the following words of Elder Orson Pratt:

Have you not read, in the New Testament, that Jesus Christ was the first-born of every creature? From this reading it would seem that he was the oldest of the whole human family, that is, so far as his birth in the spirit world is concerned. How long ago since that birth took place is not revealed; it might have been unnumbered millions of years for aught we know. But we do know that he was born and was the oldest of the family of spirits.... Does this refer to birth of the body of flesh and bones? By no means, for there were hundreds of millions who were born upon our earth before the body of flesh and bones was born whom we call Jesus. How is it, then, that he is our elder brother? We must go back to the previous birth, before the foundation of this earth; we have to go back to past ages, to the period when he was begotten of the Father among the great family of spirits.[2]

In addition, the First Presidency and Council of the Twelve Apostles, on June 30, 1916, made the following comments about the status of our Redeemer and our relationship to him as our Elder Brother in a doctrinal pronouncement:

> There is no impropriety, therefore, in speaking of Jesus Christ as the Elder Brother of the rest of human kind.... Let it not be forgotten, however, that He is essentially greater than any and all others by reason (1) of His seniority as the oldest or firstborn; (2) of His unique status in the flesh as the offspring of a mortal mother and of an immortal, or resurrected and glorified, Father; (3) of His selection and foreordination as the one and only Redeemer and Savior of the race, and (4) of His transcendent sinlessness.[3]

And in order that no Latter-day Saint might be mistaken in our understanding of the Savior's relationship to us mortals, the First Presidency added the following caution:

> Jesus Christ is not the Father of the spirits who have taken or yet shall take bodies upon this earth, for He is one of them. He is The Son, as they are sons or daughters of Elohim.[4]

Not only is the Savior our Elder Brother and the Firstborn Spirit of our Father in Heaven, but in mortality He was also the literal Son of our Father in Heaven. As quoted previously, the First Presidency has stated that Jesus Christ "in the flesh" was the son "of a mortal mother and of an immortal, or resurrected and glorified Father." (See also: Luke 1:35.) Elder Bruce R. McConkie explained the matter further, pointing out that Christ "was born into this world as the Son of Mary, inheriting from her the power of mortality, and as the Son of the "Man of Holiness [our Father in Heaven]," inheriting from Him the powers of immortality." Of this fact, President Brigham Young has conclusively stated:

> When the time came that his first-born [in the spirit], the Savior, should come into the world and take a tabernacle, the Father came himself and favored that spirit with a tabernacle instead of letting any other man do it. The Savior was begotten by the Father of his spirit, by the same Being who is the Father of our spirits, and that is all the organic difference between Jesus Christ and you and me.[5]

Christ Progressed in a Similar Manner as Did Our Father in Heaven

From pre-mortality to immortality Jesus Christ progressed on an eternal path of perfection and grace similar to that which our Father in Heaven had done. Of this similarity of progression between God the Father and God the Son, the Prophet Joseph Smith powerfully proclaimed during his last and greatest sermon, the King Follett Discourse, the following profound insights:

> When you climb up a ladder, you must begin at the bottom, and ascend step by step, until you arrive at the top; and so it is with the principles of the Gospel—you must begin with the first, and go on until you learn all the principles of exaltation. But it will be a great while after you have passed through the veil before you will have learned them. It is not all to be comprehended in this world; it will be a great work to learn our salvation and exaltation even beyond the grave....
>
> I wish I was in a suitable place to tell it, and that I had the trump of an archangel, so that I could tell the story in such a manner that persecution would cease for ever. What did Jesus say? (Mark it, Elder Rigdon!) The Scriptures inform us that Jesus said, As the Father hath power in Himself, even so hath the Son power—to do what? Why, what the Father did. The answer is obvious—in a manner to lay down His body and take it up again. Jesus, what are you going to do? To lay down my life as my Father did, and take it up again (see John 5:19).... I do the things I saw my Father do when worlds came rolling into existence. My Father worked out His kingdom with fear and trembling, and I must

do the same; and when I get my kingdom, I shall present it to my father, so that he may obtain kingdom upon kingdom, and it will exalt him in glory. He will then take a higher exaltation, and I will take his place, and thereby become exalted myself. So that Jesus treads in the tracks of his Father, and inherits what God did before; and God is thus glorified and exalted in the salvation and exaltation of all his children. . . .[6]

Likewise, Elder Bruce R. McConkie has written that in mortality Jesus Christ received "not of the fulness at the first, but went from grace to grace until. . .he gained the fulness of all things."[7] And just as Christ now has all truth, power, and knowledge, and is infinite in all his attributes and powers and has given a law unto all things, so we must also progress "from grace to grace" and "from one small degree to another" if we ever intend to become like him and to reside where he now dwells in heaven. In reference to this the Prophet Joseph Smith has proclaimed:

Here, then, is eternal life—to know the only wise and true God; and you have got to learn how to be Gods yourselves and to be kings and priests to God, the same as all Gods have done before you, namely, by going from one small degree to another, and from a small capacity to a great one, from grace to grace, from exaltation to exaltation, until you attain to the resurrection of the dead, and are able to dwell in everlasting burnings, and to sit in glory, as do those who sit enthroned in everlasting power. And I want you to know that God, in the last days, while certain individuals are proclaiming his name, is not trifling with you or me.[8]

CHAPTER SIX

The Development of Our Spirit In the Pre-Mortal Existence

The World We Lived on in Our Pre-Mortal Existence

As spirit children of our Father in Heaven, we lived in pre-mortality upon a tangible, celestialized world. Without doubt the surroundings of this celestial world were very pleasant, for it had already passed through its various stages of existence and had thus become "more perfect than this earth," being "sanctified and glorified as the residence and world where God resides."[1] Living on this sancitifed world with our Father in Heaven, we were able to enjoy the full fruition of His holy influence and inspiration.[2]

Of this celestial world where our pre-mortal spirits resided, Elder Orson Pratt has stated:

Where did we exist before we came here? With God. Where does he exist? In the place John denominated heaven. What do we understand heaven to be? Not the place described by our Christian friends, beyond the bounds of time and space, for there is no such place, there never was, nor ever will be; but I mean a tangible world, a heaven that is perfect, a heaven with materials that have been organized and put together, sanctified and glorified as the residence and world where God resides. Born there? Yes, we were born there. Even our great Redeemer, whose death and sufferings we are this afternoon celebrating, was born up in yonder world before he was born of the Virgin Mary. . . .[3]

Once we dwelt in the presence of our Father; once we were enabled to lift our songs of praise in the celestial world,

61

from which we emigrated; once we dwelt in the society of an innumerable convention of angels, upon a world that had passed through its stages, its ordeals, the same as this world is passing through its various mutations. That celestial world from whence we came, is more perfect than this earth, it is organized after a celestial order, a higher order and glorified by the presence of immortal, glorified, celestial beings. That is our home, from that world we came.[4]

Some Spirits Progressed Further in Pre-Mortality Than Did Others

From the time we were begotten upon a tangible celestialized world as "spirit children" of our Father in Heaven we were endowed with free agency and subjected to the laws of eternal progression. Throughout this spirit existence in pre-mortality—which undoubtedly was an infinitely long one—we were all taught and given experiences in various administrative capacities.[5] As a result, like on this earth, there were some spirits who so exercised their free agency and so conformed to eternal laws that they advanced to higher stations than did others.[6] Those spirits who advanced much higher, or in other words progressed much further in the pre-mortal existence than did others have been referred to in scripture as the "more intelligent" or the "noble and great ones." (Abra. 3:19, 22) Regarding this fact that some spirits progressed further in pre-mortality than did others, Elder William E. Berrett has written:

In that pre-earth life, man exercised freedom of will, was allowed his free agency, was subject to laws of progression, and did progress or retrogress in varied degree according to capacity, intelligence and obedience to law. The ancient patriarch, Abraham, whose writings have been restored, in part, was shown a vision of the pre-earth life. After showing to Abraham the varied orders of created world, some greater than others, the Lord said:

"...if there be two spirits, and one shall be more intelligent than the other, yet these two spirits, notwithstanding one is more intelligent than the other, have no beginning; they existed before, they shall have no end, they shall exist after, for they are gnolaum, or eternal.

And the Lord said unto me: These two facts do exist, one being more intelligent than the other; there shall be another more intelligent than they; I am the Lord thy God, I am more intelligent than they all.

The Lord thy God sent his angel to deliver thee from the hands of the priest of Elkenah.

I dwell in the midst of them all; I now, therefore, have come down unto thee to deliver unto thee the works which my hands have made, wherein my wisdom excelleth them all, for I rule in the heavens above, and in the earth beneath, in all wisdom and prudence, over all the intelligences thine eyes have seen from the beginning; I came down in the beginning in the midst of all the intelligences thou hast seen." (Abraham 3:18-21) [7]

Additionally, Elder Orson F. Whitney, an apostle, has stated:

In the "Book of Abraham" it is written:

"Now the Lord had shown unto me, Abraham, the intelligences that were organized before the world was; and among all these there were many of the noble and great ones.

And God saw these souls that they were good, and he stood in the midst of them, and he said: These I will make my rulers; for he stood among those that were spirits, and he saw that they were good; and he said unto me: Abraham, thou art one of them; thou wast chosen before thou wast born.

And there stood one among them that was like unto God, and he said unto those who were with him: We will go down, for there is space there, and we will take of these materials, and we will make an earth whereon these may dwell;

And we will prove them herewith, to see if they will do all things whatsoever the Lord, their God, shall command them;

And they who keep their first estate shall be added upon; and they who keep not their first estate shall not have glory in the same kingdom with those who keep their first estate; and they who keep their second estate shall have glory added upon their heads for ever and ever. (Abraham 3:22-26)

Abraham had been shown the pre-existent spirits of the human race, waiting for an earth to be made, that they might come upon it and pass through a mortal probation. Here they were to obtain bodies, thus becoming "souls," capable of endless increase and everlasting progression. They were to be tested as to their willingness to do whatever the Lord might require of them, and undergo experiences for their further education and development. All were "good," but some were better, some nobler and greater than others; and because of their superior merit and larger capacity, they were to be made "rulers" over the rest.[8]

Although some spirits did, in fact, progress further in pre-mortality than did others, it should be remembered that our Father in Heaven still considers all His "spirit children"—whether they still are spirits or are now mortals, or whether they be small or great—very precious in his sight, for we will always be His "children." As has been written in a Church magazine:

In a modern revelation, it is said that every spirit was innocent in the beginning. (D&C 93:38.) This truth indicates that each person is given a start on the way to eternal perfection. The fact that there were differences among the sons and daughters of God in pre-mortality does not suggest that all are not considered precious in his sight. It does mean, however, that he will and does give them opportunities for development in earth-life commensurate with their capacities. He looks upon the apparent superiority of some spirits over others, as given in the following remarks by Elder Parley P. Pratt:

"Although some eternal intelligences may be superior to others, and although some are more noble, and consequently are elected to fill certain useful and necessary offices for the good of others, yet the greater and the less may both be innocent, and both be justified, and be useful, each in their own capacity; if each magnify their own calling, and act in their own capacity, it is all right." (JD, 1:258.)[9]

The Election and Foreordination of Some Spirits

Because some spirits progressed further in the pre-mortal existence than did others, they were eventually "elected" (or "chosen") and "foreordained" (or "set-apart") above other spirits in pre-mortality to receive "certain blessings" and to perform "certain works" upon their entrance into this world and throughout their lives hereafter.[10] Concerning this choice "election and foreordination" of some of the "noble and great" spirits in pre-mortality, Elder William Berrett has written the following:

> Not only do we know that man existed before the earth was organized, but the revelations also point out that some were called and ordained, while yet in the spirit world for particular labors to be later performed upon the earth. They were like architects and engineers selected to erect a building before ever a shovelful of earth is turned. Abraham, the great patriarch records:
>
> "Now the Lord has shown unto me, Abraham, the intelligences that were organized before the world was; and among all these there were many of the noble and great ones;
>
> "And God saw these souls that they were good, and he stood in the midst of them, and he said: These I will make my rulers; for he stood among those that were spirits, and he saw that they were good; and he said unto me: Abraham, thou art one of them; thou was chosen before thou was born. (Abraham 3:22-23.)"[11]

In a detailed examination of the doctrine of "election" and "foreordination" Elder Robert L. Millet, a Latter-day Saint author, has expertly put together the following discourse:

Election:

> The doctrine of election has its basis in the organizational councils in the pre-earth existence. Brigham Young and Willard Richards taught that "God has chosen or elected certain individuals to certain blessings, or to the performance of certain works...." There is much evidence, for example, to indicate that certain individuals were called or elected to come to earth through certain blood lines, as a consequence of faithfulness in pre-mortal life. Elder Parley P. Pratt explained:
>
> "We read much in the Bible in relation to a choice or *election,* on the part of Deity, towards intelligences in His government on earth, whereby some were chosen to fill

stations very different from others. And this election not only affected the individuals thus chosen, but their posterity for long generations, or even for ever.

"It may be enquired where this election first originated, and upon what principle a just and impartial God exercises the elective franchise. We will go back to the earliest knowledge we have of the existence of intelligences.

"Among the intelligences that existed in the beginning, some were more intelligent than others, or, in other words, more noble; and God said to Abraham, 'These I will make my rulers!' God said unto Abraham, 'Thou art one of them; thou wast chosen before thou wast born.'

"...when He [God] speaks of nobility, He simply means an election made, and an office or a title conferred, on the principle of superiority of intellect, or nobleness of action, or of capacity to act. And *when this election, with its titles, dignities, and estates, includes the unborn posterity of a chosen man,* as in the case of Abraham, Isaac, and Jacob, *it is with a view of the noble spirits of the eternal world coming through their lineage,* and being taught in the commandments of God. Hence the Prophets, Kings, Priests, Patriarchs, Apostles, and even Jesus Christ, were included in the election of Abraham, and of his seed, as manifested to him in an eternal covenant...."

It is clear, then, that those who came through the Abrahamic lineage were called and elected to do so, and will be the means of blessing the world. This concept was taught to the Saints in the early history of the Church; they were informed that "God elected or chose the children of Israel to be His peculiar people, and to them belong the covenants and promises and the blessings received by the Gentiles come through the covenants to Abraham and his seed...and thus the house of Israel became the ministers of salvation to the Gentiles; and this is what the house of Israel was elected unto, not only their own salvation, but through them salvation to all others...."

It is through those called and elected in the organizational councils that the Priesthood is to be given, should they prove worthy on earth. One of the great promises of God to Abraham was that the Priesthood would continue in his seed throughout eternity. Parley P. Pratt continued his discourse on the doctrine of election in the flesh:

"In this peculiar lineage, and in no other should all the nations be blessed. From the days of Abraham until now, if the people of any country, age or nation, have been blessed with the blessings peculiar to the everlasting covenant of the Gospel, its sealing powers, Priesthood, and ordinances, it has been through the ministry of that lineage, and the keys of Priesthood held by the lawful heirs according to the flesh...no man can hold the keys of Priesthood or of Apostleship, to bless or administer salvation to the nations, unless he is a literal descendant of Abraham, Isaac, and Jacob.

"Knowing of the covenants and promises made to the fathers, as I now know them, and the rights of heirship to the Priesthood, as manifested in the election of God, I would never receive any man as an Apostle or a Priest, holding the keys of restoration, to bless the nations, while he claimed to be any other lineage than Israel."

Foreordination

Whereas the doctrine of election has reference to the fact that all persons (men and women) who perform timely works and missions were chosen to perform those works in the organizational councils, Joseph Smith taught that "every *man* who has a calling to minister to the inhabitants of the world was *ordained* to that very purpose in the Grand Council of heaven before the world was." Foreordination thus consists of a more specific aspect of the principle of election, in which certain men were set apart and ordained to perform various roles in the Priesthood. The scriptures plainly teach of the foreordination of great Priesthood leaders. Peter referred to Christ as "a lamb without blemish and without spot: who verily was *foreordained before the foundation of the world....*" Wilford Woodruff spoke in a similar vein of other Prophets: "The Prophet Joseph taught us that father Adam was the first man on the earth to whom God gave the keys of the everlasting priesthood. He held the keys of the presidency, and was the first man who did hold them. Noah stood next to him, he being the father of all living in his day, as Adam was in his day. *These two men were the first who received the priesthood in the eternal worlds, before the worlds were formed."* In speaking of the council of the noble and great ones, Abraham said: "And God saw these souls that they were good, and he stood in the midst of them, and he said: These I will make my rulers; for he stood among those that were spirits, and he saw that they were good; and he said unto me: Abraham, thou art one of them; *thou wast chosen before thou wast born."* To the Prophet Jeremiah the word of the Lord came: *"Before I formed thee in the belly I knew thee; and before thou camest forth out of the womb I sanctified thee, and I ordained thee a prophet unto the nations."* Joseph Smith, the Latter-day Seer, was unquestionably among the noble and great foreordained to a mighty mission in mortality. In speaking of Joseph, President George Q. Cannon said: "He, therefore, was a Prophet, Seer and Revelator before he was ordained in the flesh. Did you ever think of it? Brother Joseph Smith was a Prophet, Seer and Revelator before he ever received any Priesthood in the flesh...."

Foreordination to Priesthood offices and callings is not limited to the Prophets of God. All who receive Priesthood in mortality were called to that position before the earth was formed. Joseph Fielding Smith said: "In regard to the holding of the priesthood in pre-existence, I will say that there was an organization there just as well as an organization here, and men there held authority. Men chosen to positions of trust in the spirit world held priesthood...."

Perhaps the most beautiful and detailed description of foreordination of Priesthood bearers was given by a *Book of Mormon* Prophet. After preaching a great discourse to the people concerning the plan of salvation and the role of the Savior in that plan, Alma continued:

"And again, my brethren, I would cite your minds forward to the time when the Lord God gave these commandments unto his children; and I would that ye should remember that the Lord God ordained priests, after his holy order, which was after the order of his Son, to teach these things to the people.

"And those priests were ordained after the order of his Son, in a manner that thereby the people might know in what manner to look forward to his Son for redemption.

"And this is the manner after which they were ordained—being called and prepared from the foundation of the world according to the foreknowledge of God, on account of their exceeding faith and good works; in the first place being left to choose good or evil; therefore they having chosen good, and exercising exceeding great faith, are called with a holy calling, yea, with that holy calling which was prepared with, and according to, a preparatory redemption for such.

"And thus they have been called to this holy calling on account of their faith, while others would reject the Spirit of God on account of the hardness of their hearts and blindness of their minds, while, if it had not been for this they might have had as great privilege as their brethren.

"Or in fine, in the first place they were on the same standing with their brethren; thus this holy calling being prepared from the foundation of the world for such as would not harden their hearts, being in and through the atonement of the Only Begotten Son, who was prepared.

"And thus being called by this holy calling, and ordained unto the high priesthood of the holy order of God, to teach his commandments unto the children of men, that they also might enter into his rest—

"This high priesthood being after the order of his Son, which order was from the foundation of the world; or in other words, being without beginning of days or end of years, being prepared from eternity to all eternity, according to his foreknowledge of all things

"Now they were ordained after this manner—being called with a holy calling, and ordained with a holy ordinance, and taking upon them the high priesthood of the holy order, which calling, and ordinance, and high priesthood, is without beginning or end—

"Thus they become high priests forever, after the order of the Son, the Only Begotten of the Father, who is without beginning of days or end of years, who is full of grace, equity and truth. And thus it is. Amen." (Alma 13:1-9)

After studying these nine verses carefully, the following points seem to take on great meaning: First, God has chosen men, and ordained them to the Priesthood after the order of His Son, to teach the people concerning the Atonement and the path back into the presence of God. These men were ordained after the order of the Son of God, because it is only to Christ that man may look for redemption and eternal life. Second, these men were called, prepared, and ordained in the pre-earth councils, according to the foreknowledge of God. This calling and ordination came because of their exceeding faith and good works in the ages preceding mortality; that is to say, these brethren indicated a faithful and valiant spirit in following the path of greatest truth, and thus exercised their agency so as to be added upon. Third, these men, called and ordained before the foundations of the earth, came to earth and were left to themselves, either to choose good or evil; they had the right to exercise agency once again. Having chosen good, and once more shown great faith, they are ordained on earth to a holy calling in the High Priesthood. Fourth, others of their brethren who were called, elected, and ordained with them in the organizational councils have come to earth, rejected the promptings of the Holy Spirit, and therefore turned away from the light of the Gospel and subsequent calling and ordination to the Priesthood in mortality. In the beginning (in the world of spirits), all of these men were on the same standing, and thus had the same opportunity for advancement and progression. But because of the power of the flesh, many did not live worthy of Priesthood and its rights. Finally, these men are ordained priests after the order of the Son of God, which calling (to the Melchizedek Priesthood) and ordinance (the laying on of hands) are eternal and most holy. They are given these rights in order that they might bless the world, and ultimately bring all the pure in heart into the rest of God, or the fulness of His glory.[12]

Latter-day Saints should also understand that "foreordination" is not "predestination." For although God may appoint certain of His spirit children to do specific tasks upon the earth, man still has at all times his free agency to either reject God's will or to follow it. This is made clear by the Savior in a revelation to the Prophet Joseph Smith, who was warned in these words:

For although a man may have many revelations, and have power to do many mighty works, yet if he boasts in his own strength, and sets at naught the counsels of God, and follows after the dictates of his own will and carnal desires, he must fall and incur the vengeance of a just God upon him....

Behold, thou art Joseph, and thou wast chosen to do the work of the Lord, but because of transgression, if thou art not aware thou wilt fall.

But remember, God is merciful, therefore, repent of that which thou hast done which is contrary to the commandment which I gave you, and thou art still chosen, and art again called to the work.

Except thou do this, thou shalt be delivered up and become as other men, and have no more gift. (D & C 3:4, 9-11.)

In conclusion, it should be remembered that even though our Father in Heaven can "see the end of" our "earthly career even from the first"...because of His long "acquaintanceship and foreknowledge" of our character,..."yet that knowledge" of His is not a "compelling force" upon us, for we still exercise our own freedom in choosing good or evil. In reference to this subject the following comments appear from a Church lesson manual:

> Elder Talmage expressed the belief that God's knowledge of his sons and daughters in the pre-earth life was very extensive. He could "see the end of their earthly career even from the first." (Talmage, *The Articles of Faith,* p. 191.) He also wrote: "Everyone of us was known by name and character to the Father, who is 'the God of the spirits of all flesh' (Numbers 16:22; 27:16), in our antemortal or primeval childhood; and from among the hosts of His unembodied children God chose for special service on earth such as were best suited to the accomplishment of His purposes." (Talmage, *The Vitality of Mormonism,* p. 229.) Notwithstanding this acquaintanceship and foreknowledge, Elder Talmage wrote: "God's knowledge of spiritual and of human nature enables Him to conclude with certainty as to the actions of any of His children under given conditions; yet that knowledge is not of compelling force upon the creature." (Talmage, *The Articles of Faith,* p. 191.)
> The Prophet Joseph Smith was foreordained to one of the most important missions of this life. That even he could have failed to fulfill this calling is evidenced in a revelation given in 1830 to Joseph Smith and Sidney Rigdon. (D & C 35:18.) Referring to Joseph Smith we read the following: *"...if he abide in me,* and if not, another will I plant in his stead." (Italics added.)[13]

CHAPTER SEVEN

The Council In Heaven

The Head of the Gods Call a Council of the Gods

None of us as mortals know how long we existed as spirit children of our Father in Heaven before entering this world. However, it is apparent that sometime during our pre-mortal spirit existence that an "organization" or "Council of...Gods," in which our Father in Heaven and Elder Brother Jesus Christ were probably included, drew up a plan to arrange for the creation and peopling of this world and of other worlds yet to come.[1] Regarding this meeting or "Council of the Gods," Elder Robert Millet has conclusively written the following:

> The first glimpse we get into a specific preparation for earth-life is what is called in scripture "The Council of the Gods." It was at this council, held near unto the residence of Elohim, that plans were drawn up and final decisions made regarding the creation and redemption of this world and others. Joseph Smith said: "In the beginning, the head of the Gods called a *council of the Gods;* and they came together and concocted a plan to create the world and people it." Regarding the circumstances of this meeting, Orson F. Whitney wrote:

> In solemn council sat the Gods;
> From Kolob's height supreme.
> Celestial light blazed forth afar
> O'er countless kokaubeam:

73

> And faintest tinge, the fiery fringe
> Of that resplendent day.
> 'Luminated the dark abysmal realm
> Where earth in chaos lay.

Joseph Smith explained that "the grand councilors sat at the head in yonder heavens and contemplated the creation of the worlds which were created at the time." We are uncertain as to specific names and/or personalities in attendance at this great planning session, though it is highly probable that Elohim and Jehovah were among those present.[2]

God Assembles His Spirit Children for a Great Council in Heaven

Sometime after the "Council of the Gods" had discussed and planned the future creation and peopling of this world and others, our Father in Heaven assembled together all His spirit children in a great general conference, the "Council in Heaven." [3]

The purpose of this Council in Heaven was to provide the spirit children of our Eternal Father the opportunity to "consider" for acceptance or rejection[4] the plan which the Council of the Gods had arrived at as to the manner in which the earth should be peopled and eternal salvation and exaltation should be perpetuated.[5] Of our attendence at this Council in Heaven, Elder Robert Millet has said:

> Some time before coming to earth it appears from scripture that all of the spirit children of Elohim met in a great general conference to consider the plans to be followed in peopling the newly created earth(s), and providing a program whereby all could possibly return to the Celestial home as glorified and perfected souls.[6]

And Elder Bruce R. McConkie has written that the Prophet Joseph Smith when speaking of "the grand council in heaven" stated that it was at this meeting in which "those destined 'to minister to the inhabitants of the world' were 'ordained' to their respective callings."[7] Therefore, the Council in Heaven was indeed an occasion for accomplishing many diversified tasks of eternal importance.

The Sons of God Shout for Joy

At the outset of the Council in Heaven, our Eternal Father informed all His "spirit children" of His intention to create this world and to place man upon it so that His spirit children could thereby "obtain tabernacles and in those tabernacles obey laws of life, and with them again be exalted among the Gods."[8]

After hearing this good news and later witnessing our Father in Heaven begin the work of laying "the foundations of the earth," we as His spirit children became so elated and excited over the prospect of our gaining a body and thereby eventually becoming more like our majestic Eternal Father, that we all "shouted for joy."[9] Of this occasion the scriptures state:

> Where wast thou when I laid the foundations of the earth? declare, if thou hast understanding....
> When the morning stars sang together, and all the sons of God shouted for joy? (Job 38:4,7.)

Whether the spirit "sons (and daughters) of God shouted for joy" by entertaining musical instruments or even by engaging in dancing, we do not know; "but one thing is certain, they had great joy and the heavens resounded with their shouts."[10]

As for the reason why the pre-mortal "sons of God" shouted for joy, Elder Orson Pratt has said that they did so "because there was a beautiful habitation being built, so that they could get (mortal) tabernacles...for their spirits to dwell in":

> The *Sons* of God, recollect, shouted for joy, because there was a beautiful habitation being built, so that they could get tabernacles, and dwell thereon; they expected the time—they looked forward to the period; and it was joyful to them to reflect, that the creation was about being formed, the corner stone of it was laid, on which they might, in their times, and in their seasons, and in their generations, go forth and receive tabernacles for their spirits to dwell in. Do you bring it home to yourselves, brethren and sisters? Do you realize that you and I were there? Can you bring it to your minds that you and I were among that happy number that shouted for joy when this creation was made? Says one, I don't recollect it. No wonder! for your recollection is taken from you, because you are in a tabernacle that is earthly; and all this is right and necessary.[11]

In addition, Elder J. Preston Creer, an early author and member of the Church, has stated that as pre-mortal spirits we all realized that only by coming to earth and gaining a mortal body for our spirits to dwell in could we ever become like our Father in Heaven:

> God desired that we should become like unto him—fathers as well as sons; kings as well as subjects; creators as well as things created. This righteous desire enjoyed alike by man and by his creator, could be materialized only by coming to earth and taking upon ourselves bodies wherein our spirits might gain experience. We were to emerge from beneath divine protection, and be thrown into the midst of sin and degradation. We were to become acquainted with grief, and to be known as men of pain, and sorrow. Yet the knowledge that we should some day be redeemed and exalted in the presence of our Maker, banished our fears, filled our souls with hope, and afforded us such gladness, that in our delight, we sang and shouted for joy.[12]

And Elder Orson F. Whitney, an early Apostle of the Church, has specifically concluded why we as pre-earthly spirits needed a mortal body in which to dwell and progress throughout eternity:

> Man needed experience in mortality—in the midst of rudimental conditions, that he might attain to higher wisdom, and greater worthiness. He also needed a body for purposes of increase and progression, both in time and eternity. The spirit without the body is imperfect; it cannot propagate, and it cannot go on to glory. The fall of man gave bodies to the spirits awaiting them, with further opportunities for education and expansion.
>
> "The great principle of happiness," says Joseph Smith, "consists in having a body. The Devil has no body, and herein is his punishment. All beings who have bodies have power over those who have not."[13]

God's Plan of Sacrifice and Salvation is Accepted Over Lucifer's Plan of Forced Redemption

After our Father in Heaven had revealed to His spirit children in the Council in Heaven that He had undertaken to lay the foundations of a world upon which they could eventually obtain mortal bodies, "the question then arose" as to "how, and upon what principle,...the salvation, exaltation, and eternal glory of God's sons" should "be brought about."[14]

It appears that at this time in the Council in Heaven "certain plans (of salvation and exaltation) had been proposed...," and that "a full discussion of (those plans) and principles" along with the declaration of the Father's will" for a plan of "sacrifice and salvation," was clearly discussed among all the spirit children of our Eternal Father.[15]

Of our Father in Heaven's proposed plan of sacrifice and salvation, Elder Bruce R. McConkie has written:

> Ordinarily, perhaps, when the saints speak of the *council in heaven,* they have in mind the solemn session (at which, apparently, all of the pre-existent hosts were present) when the Father made formal announcement of his plan of redemption and salvation. It was then explained that his spirit children would go down to earth, gain bodies of flesh and blood, be tried and tested in all things, and have opportunity by obedience to come back again to the Eternal Presence. It was then explained that one of the spirit children of the Father would be chosen to be the Redeemer and work out the infinite and eternal atonement. And it was then that the Father sent forth the call which said in substance and effect: Whom shall I send to be my Son in mortality? Who will go down, be born with life in himself, and work out the great atoning sacrifice by which immortality will come to all men and eternal life be assured to the obedient?[16]

Following the presentation of our Father in Heaven's plan of "sacrifice and salvation" and His final question of "Whom shall I send"[17] into mortality to work out the atoning sacrifice for the benefit of all mankind, our Eternal Father's Firstborn Son, our Savior Jesus Christ, spoke forth and in effect said, "Here am I, send me,[18] I will be thy Son and will follow thy plan; and 'Father, thy will be done, and glory be thine forever.' "[19] This statement by our Savior evinced such humility and obedience to the principles of eternal truth and light that our Father in Heaven was very much pleased with him.

However, Jesus Christ was only one of two mighty spirit sons of our Father in Heaven who on that occasion volunteered his services to carry out the infinite and atoning sacrifice of the plan of salvation. The other spirit son of our Father in Heaven who offered his services was "Lucifer," a spirit who had been born in the morning of pre-mortality but who had continually been "a liar from the beginning."[20]

After Jesus Christ had humbly volunteered his services in carrying out the infinite atonement and plan of salvation of our Heavenly Father, Lucifer sinisterly stepped forward and diabolically proclaimed before God our Father and His spirit children an evil plan of "forced redemption with no free agency" as the one that should be accepted and followed. Needless to say, Lucifer's plan was exactly contrary to the will of our Eternal Father.[21]

As to the status of Lucifer in the pre-mortal existence and the plan of "forced redemption" that he proposed, Elder Bruce R. McConkie has also stated:

> [Lucifer, also called the Devil, was] a spirit son of God who was born in the morning of pre-existence. (D&C 76:25-26.) Endowed with agency, the free power of choice, he chose the evil part from the beginning, thus placing himself in eternal opposition to the divine will. He was "a liar from the beginning." (D&C 93:25.)
>
> Obviously he gained for himself great executive and administrative ability and had a sufficiently compelling personality to influence for ill a myraid host of other spirit offspring of the Father. His position was one of great power and authority. He was "an angel of God" who "became a devil, having sought that which was evil before God." (2 Nephi 2:17; D&C 76:25.)
>
> When the plan of salvation was presented—the plan whereunder the spirit children of the Father would be enabled to gain tangible bodies and, if faithful in all things, progress to a like status with their Father—and when the need for a Redeemer was explained, Satan offered to come into the world as the Son of God and be the Redeemer. "Behold, here am I, send me," he said. "I will be thy son." But then, as always, he was in opposition to the full plan of the Father, and so he sought to amend and change the terms of salvation; he sought to deny men their agency and to dethrone God. "I will redeem all mankind, that one soul shall not be lost, and surely I will do it; wherefore give me thine honor," he continued. (Moses 4:14.)[22]

Other General Authorities of the Church have also spoken about Lucifer and his plan of "forced redemption with no free agency" as well as his selfish desire for "the honor and glory that belong only to our Father in Heaven." Elder Orson F. Whitney has said for example:

Lucifer, an angel "in authority in the presence of God," would fain have been selected for (a) mighty mission; but his scheme for human redemption was of a compulsory character, destructive of the free agency of man. Moreover, this "Son of the Morning" had become darkened to that degree that he demanded, in recompense for his proposed service, the honor and glory that belong only to the Highest. Therefore was he rejected....[23]

Likewise, President John Taylor has stated:

Lucifer wanted to introduce a plan contrary to the will of his Father, and then wanted His honor, and said: "I will save every soul of man, wherefore give me thine honor." He wanted to go contrary to the will of his Father, and pre- sumptuously sought to deprive man of his free agency, thus making him a serf, and placing him in a position in which it was impossible for him to obtain that exaltation which God designed should be man's, through obedience to the law which He had suggested; and again, Lucifer wanted the honor and power of his Father, to enable him to carry out principles which were contrary to the Father's wish.[24]

And Elder Orson Pratt has also concluded:

Lucifer...proposed a plan by which he would redeem all mankind, that not one soul should be lost. But his plan was rejected, because it destroyed the agency of man, being contrary to God's plan; for he desires that all intelligent beings shall be free in the exercise of their agency. Because his plan was rejected, Lucifer rebelled....[25]

After Satan had selfishly and evilly proposed his diabolical plan of "forced redemption," our Father in Heaven rejected his offer and chose His Beloved Son Jesus Christ to be our Redeemer and Savior. Of this selection event our Lord has said:

And the Lord said: Whom shall I send? And one answered like unto the Son of Man: Here am I, send me. And another answered and said: Here am I, send me. And the Lord said: I will send the first.

And the second was angry, and kept not his first estate, and, at that day, many followed after him. (Abraham 3:27-28)

CHAPTER EIGHT

The War In Heaven

Lucifer Rebels Against God and Becomes Satan

After our Father in Heaven had chosen Jesus Christ to be the Redeemer and Savior of this world, Lucifer, who's own selfish intents and evil plan of "forced redemption" had been rejected by God, became indignant and "openly rebelled" and fought against our Eternal Father "and His authority and all the truths of eternity."[1]

Because of his rebellion or "open defiance" against our Father in Heaven and his desire to destroy the free agency "which God had given to man," Lucifer became "Satan, yea even the devil, the father of all lies, to deceive and to blind men, and to lead them captive at his will" down to hell.[2]

Satan Leads a Third of the Hosts of Heaven to War Against God

When Satan made the decision to openly rebel and therefore "war" against our Father in Heaven, he did not intend to wage his battle alone. Throughout the pre-mortal existence, Lucifer, as a mighty spirit son of our Eternal Father, had "gained for himself great executive and administrative ability and had a sufficiently compelling personality to influence for ill a myriad host of other spirit offspring of the Father."[3]

Therefore, when Satan decided to rebel against our Eternal Father, he zealously labored to convince as many of the spirit sons and daughters of God as he could to join him in his rebellion. Eventually, Satan succeeded in drawing away from our

Heavenly Father one third of the spirit hosts of Heaven who were originally assigned to partake of mortal life on this earth. These rebellious spirits then joined Satan in his "war" against God. Concerning this event, Elder J. Preston Creer, a Latter-day Saint author has written:

> [Satan] zealously...labored with all the powers of his soul; arguing, persuading, influencing whosoever desired to be serfs, rather than men endowed with the inalienable right of absolute freedom to choose between good and evil. With his mighty eloquence and great personality, he succeeded in drawing into his mesh of misery and woe one-third of the hosts of heaven[4] [that were destined for life on this earth...[5]].

Also, Elder Orson Pratt has stated:

> [Satan] did not repent of his rebellion, nor of the wicked proposition; but he sought to turn away the family of heaven—the family of spirits that were in the presence of God—he sought to turn them away and convert them to his plan. But he did not succeed. He did succeed in leading away about one-third part of that great family of spirits, because of their agency. They hearkened to his proposition; they thought it would be a very great and important thing to destroy the agency of man in the future creation that was about to be made, and to redeem them all in their sins, and consequently they joined with this rebellious character; hence came the fallen angels.[6]

After Satan had succeeded in persuading one-third of our Father in Heaven's spirit children to rebel and wage war against their God, a "war in heaven" ensued.[7] On the one side, our Father in Heaven commissioned "Michael the Archangel," known to Latter-day Saints as the man, Adam (who except for Jesus Christ was the second most intelligent, powerful and mighty spirit son of our Father in the pre-mortal existence[8]), to lead the remaining two-thirds of His faithful spirit children to fight "against Satan... and his followers and to cast them out of His presence." On the other side, Satan "the dragon," and "his angels"[9] fought to destroy the agency of man and "to modify the Father's plan so that [exaltation and] salvation would come automatically to all who passed through mortality."[10] In regard to this "war in heaven" which took place between Michael the Archangel (in behalf of our Father in Heaven and His Son Jesus Christ) and Satan, whom we know as the Devil, the scriptures inform us that:

> There was war in heaven: Michael and his angels fought against the dragon; and the dragon fought and his angels,
> And prevailed not; neither was their place found any more in heaven.
> And the great dragon was cast out, that old serpent, called the Devil, and Satan, which deceiveth the whole world: he was cast out into the earth, and his angels were cast out with him.[11]

The Literal Nature of the War in Heaven

As to the literal nature and occurrences which took place in and during the "war in heaven," very little information has been given us in either the scriptures or modern-day revelations. Perhaps the best detailed description, if true, of an occurrence which might have taken place during this event known as the "war in heaven" has been given to us by Elder Hugh Nibley, professor emeritus of ancient scripture at Brigham Young University. He has written:

> Surprisingly enough, the best documented story of a clash between Adam and Satan is the scene in heaven. One old writing with unusually good credentials that trace back to books deposited by the apostles in the first Church archives in Jerusalem is the Coptic "Discourse of the Abbaton, a sermon based on the text delivered by Timothy the Archbishop of Alexandria."
> The book belongs to the forty-day literature; and as it opens, the Lord on his last day on earth with the apostles just before his ascension asks them if there is any final request they would like to make of him—exactly as in Third Nephi 28:1. What they want most is to understand the role of Death and its horrors in God's plan for his children. To explain this the Lord tells them of the council in heaven in the preexistence where the plan of the creation is being discussed.
> There was great reluctance among the hosts to proceed with the creation of the earth, the earth itself complaining, exactly in the manner of Moses 7:48, of the filthiness and

corruption that would surely go out of her and begging to be allowed to rest from such horrors. (Fol. 10a-b.) Because of the council's reluctance to proceed, God allows the lifeless body of Adam to lie upon the earth for forty days, unwilling, without the council's approval, to let his spirit enter. (11b.) The Son of God saves the day by offering to pay the price for whatever suffering will be entailed, thus permitting "God's children to return again to their former condition." (12a.) Christ alone thus becomes the author of our earthly exist- ence; amid joy and rejoicing God calls for a book, in which he registers the names of all the "Sons of God" who are to go to earth (See Gen. 5:1ff, Fol. 12b.) This of course is the heavenly book of the generations of Adam open at the foun- dation of the earth, the book to which Enoch refers so explic- itly in Moses 6:46, 8.

In the presence of all the hosts, Adam is next made ready to take over his great assignment. He is placed on a throne and given a crown of glory and a scepter, and all the sons of God bow the knee first to God the Father and then to Adam the Father in recognition of his beginning in God's exact likeness and image. (13a.) Satan, however, refuses to comply, declaring that he is willing to worship the Father but not Adam: "It is rather he that should worship me for I arrived before he did!" (13a-b.) (See Moses 1:19: "I am the Only Begotten, worship me.") God saw that Satan, be- cause of his boundless ambition and total lack of humility, could no longer be trusted with celestial power and com- manded the angels to remove him from his office. This ordi- nance they performed with great sorrow and reluctance: They "removed the writing of authority from his hand. They took from him his armor and all the insignia of priesthood and kingship." Then with a ceremonial knife, a sickle, they inflicted upon him certain ceremonial blows of death which deprived him of his full strength forever after. (14a.) Other accounts say that after these cuts he retained only one-third of his former power, even as he was followed by one-third of the hosts.[12]

Satan and His Followers Lose the War in Heaven and Are Cast Down to the Earth

Although we are not sure what specific events took place during the "war in heaven" we do know the resultant outcome.

The scriptures tell us that Satan and his followers did, in fact, lose in the "war in heaven" and were cast down to this earth as spirit entities who would never have the chance of possessing physical bodies of flesh and bone throughout the rest of eternity.[13] Concerning this fact, President Brigham Young has said:

> In regard to the battle in heaven,...how much of a battle it was I have forgotten. I cannot relate the principal circumstances, it is so long since it happened; but I do not think it lasted very long; for when Lucifer, the son of the morning, claimed the privilege of having the control of this earth, and redeeming it, a contention arose; but I do not think it took long to cast down one-third of the hosts of heaven, as it is written in the Bible. But let me tell you that it was one-third part of the spirits who were prepared to take tabernacles upon this earth, and who rebelled against the other two-thirds of the heavenly host; and they were cast down to this world. It is written that they were cast down to the earth. They were cast down to this globe—to this terra firma that you and I walk upon, and whose atmosphere we breathe. One-third part of the spirits that were prepared for this earth rebelled against Jesus Christ, and were cast down to the earth, and they have been opposed to him from that day to this, with Lucifer at their head. He is their general—Lucifer, the son of the morning. He was once a brilliant and influential character in heaven, and we will know more about him hereafter.[14]

And Elder Orson F. Whitney has also expressed:

> The reason why Satan has no body is because he rebelled in the Eternal Councils, when the creation of this earth was considered, and a Redeemer for it chosen.... Therefore was he rejected, and, rebelling, "was thrust down from the presence of God and the Son, and was called Perdition, for the heavens wept over him." "And also a third part of the host of heaven turned he away—because of their agency." (D & C 76:25, 26; 29:36.)[15]

In addition it should be remembered that during the "war in heaven" there were no neutral spirits "any more than there are or can be neutrals in this life where choices between righteousness and unrighteousness are involved,"[16] for "He that is not with me is against me," saith the Lord, "and he that gathereth not with me scattereth abroad."[17]

As to the eternal consequences for those pre-mortal spirits who rebelled against their Father in Heaven, Elder Cleon Skousen has given us the following insight:

> Only as recently as the "pre-existence" we lost one-third of our brothers and sisters (D & C 29:36), and all of those, together with the so-called "sons of perdition" who tasted the powers of heaven but betrayed the Lord in this estate, will eventually be stripped of all their embellishments and *"return again to their own place...*because they were not willing to enjoy that which they might have received." (D & C 88:32)
>
> How terrible this experience will be for those who are cast back again into the outer regions of chaos and darkness where there is neither order, physical embodiment, opportunity for growth or any means of achieving self-realization!
>
> The Lord says this experience is so appalling and abhorrent to those who suffer it that "the end thereof, neither the place thereof, nor their torment, no man knows; neither was it revealed, neither is, neither will be revealed unto man, except to them who are made partakers thereof." (D & C 45-46)[18]

And Elder Daniel H. Ludlow has expertly summerized why it is that Satan and his followers will experience eternal torment, condemnation, and limitations:

> Some persons might feel that God the Father was unjust or unfair when he denied the right of earth life to Lucifer and his followers in consequence of their rebellion against him in heaven. However, the following principles which apply to Lucifer's predicament should be kept in mind:
>
> 1. God is a God of law and order; thus he is bound by certain divine and eternal laws. (D & C 82:10; Alma 12:32; 42:13.) One of the eternal laws by which God is bound is the law of justice which is essentially that every law has both a punishment and a blessing affixed to it; whenever a law is transgressed (or broken), a punishment or suffering must be inflicted; whenever a law is kept (or obeyed), a blessing must be given. Thus, all punishments and blessings are based (or predicated) upon disobedience or obedience to divine law. (D & C 82:10; 130:20-21.)

2. Lucifer and his followers willfully and knowingly rebelled against the plan of God, and they refused to keep the laws upon which the blessings of earth life are predicated. Thus, they literally brought upon themselves their own condemnation. They—and not God—are directly responsible for their punishment and their limitations.

3. At least one condition is worse than the punishment which was pronounced upon Lucifer (Perdition) and his followers (or "sons") of not being allowed to come upon the earth and obtain physical bodies. This more serious condition is to become a "Son of Perdition" *after* obtaining a physical body. The Lord has defined this class of "Sons of Perdition" as follows: "Thus saith the Lord concerning all those who know my power, and have been made partakers thereof, and suffered themselves through the power of the devil to be overcome, and to *deny* the truth and *defy* my power—

"They are they who are the sons of perdition, of whom I say that *it had been better for them never to have been born;*

"...Concerning whom I have said there is no forgiveness in this world nor in the world to come—..." (D & C 76:31-32, 34; Italics added; also read 35-38.)

The justice of the punishments which have come upon the two classes of sons of perdition should be obvious to the sincere seeker of truth. Lucifer and the hosts who followed him in heaven refused at the great council to accept the atonement of Jesus Christ and the other laws necessary for an earth life; thus they were denied the blessings and privileges of mortality. Cain and the others who have become sons of perdition on this earth, however, agreed in the council in heaven to accept and obey all the commandments of God; yet when they came to the earth they broke these additional covenants. Thus the punishment to be inflicted upon the *physical* sons of perdition will be more severe than the punishment meted out to Lucifer and his *spiritual* cohorts. The scriptures clearly indicate that Cain (who became a son of perdition on the earth) will rule over Lucifer (who became a son of perdition at the time of the council in heaven)—that is, Cain is more evil and wicked than Lucifer for he has broken additional promises to God. (See Moses 5:22-25.)[19]

Satan, Perhaps, Was Not the First Evil Spirit
to Rebel Against God

As far as men on this earth are concerned, evil had its beginning in our pre-mortal existence when Satan and one-third of the
spirit children designated for this earth rebelled against their
Father in Heaven.[20]

However, this does not mean that Satan and his fellow evil
spirits are the only source of evil throughout the vast concourses
of the universe. For just as our own Father in Heaven "had a
Father...who likewise had a Father..."[21] so is it possible that
throughout the numerous creations of "the Gods," other evil
spirits may have at one time or another also rebelled against
"their Deities" just as Satan, our Devil, rebelled against our Father in Heaven.

Concerning this possibility, Elder Orson Pratt has stated
that we should "not consider that the rebellion which took place
in heaven prior to this creation was the first rebellion that had
ever existed:"[22]

We do not consider that this creation on which we dwell
was the first one that was made. We do not consider that the
rebellion which took place in heaven prior to this creation
was the first rebellion that had ever existed. We do not consider that those beings who rebelled was the first ones that
ever had their agency; but we believe that God has always
been at work, from all eternity; and that the creations which
he has made are innumerable unto men. No man is capable
of conceiving of the number. And those creations were made
to be inhabited by rational, intelligent beings, having their
agency. But this seems to be the origin of evil so far as the
inhabitants intended for this earth, and who were then living
in heaven, were concerned. They had their agency; and when
I speak of the inhabitants that dwell in heaven, pertaining to
this creation, I mean the spirits of men and women. I have no
reference to the mortal tabernacles which we have received
here, but I have reference to those beings who dwell within
these tabernacles, who are intelligent, who have their
agency, who had a pre-existence, who lived before the world
was made. The inhabitants of heaven, who were selected to
come on this creation, were agents, just as much as we are.
They had a law given to them, just as much as we have. They
had penalties affixed to that law, just the same as we have.
They could keep that law given to them in heaven, just as

well as we could keep a law given to us. They could rebel against that law, because of their agency, the same as we rebel against the laws of heaven.[23]

CHAPTER NINE

The Effects of Pre-Mortality Upon Our Earthly Life

The Importance of Keeping Our First Estate

Following the "war in heaven" those spirits who remained loyal to our Father in Heaven earned for themselves the right to be born into this world and to receive mortal bodies of flesh and bone. Because of their loyalty to our Eternal Father, these faithful spirits had "kept their first estate," pre-mortality, and thus, proving themselves worthy for further advancement, had gained the right to enter into the "second estate" of mortality. In contrast, Satan and his rebellious followers did not keep "their first estate" (Jude 6) and were therefore cast out of God's presence and denied bodies of flesh and bone and the probationary experiences of mortality.[1]

It is important for us to remember that we are now here in mortality only because we "kept our first estate;" and that having proven ourselves worthy in pre-mortality of further "light and knowledge" we have been sent to earth to see if we will likewise succeed in proving ourselves faithful during this "second estate" of our eternal existence. In regard to the importance of keeping our first (and second) estates, Elder Orson F. Whitney has said:

> The "second," whom the Lord did not "send," was Lucifer, who became Satan. Of him, more anon. The "first estate" is the spirit life, lived by man prior to being placed on earth in a body of flesh and blood. In the spirit life God's children "walk by sight." The "second estate" signifies life in the flesh, where these same spirits, in mortal bodies, are required to "walk by faith," with the knowledge of the past

temporarily obscured, that their agency may be entirely free, uninfluenced by any recollection of a former experience, unless it be awakened by inspiration. Manifestly, the second estate, compared with the first, is a much greater test of integrity, and one that results, to those who overcome, in a far more glorious reward than any previously bestowed. [2]

The Covenants We Made Before Coming to Earth

Shortly after the great "Council" and subsequent "war in heaven" "much specific organization and planning were undertaken relative to mortality." It was probably at this stage of our pre-mortal existence, which the Prophet Joseph Smith termed the "first organization," that various covenants were made and entered into between our spirits and our Father in Heaven regarding our future roles on this earth. [3] Concerning the "covenants" we entered into with our Eternal Father at this latter time in our pre-mortal existence, Elder Orson Hyde, an apostle in the early days of the restoration, has stated:

We entered into a covenant with the powers celestial, before we left our former homes, that we would come here and obey the voice of the Lord, through whomsoever he might speak,...and it is not impossible that we signed the articles thereof with our own hands,—which articles may be retained in the archives above, to be presented to us when we rise from the dead, and be judged out of our own mouths, according to that which is written in the books.

We are situated here in various relations, not only to the servants of God that are given us to guide our energies, but we also stand in various relations to one another, as husband and wife, parent and child,—which relations are branches of that everlasting covenant, because they are legitimate and ordained of God. Did we covenant and agree that we would be subject to the authorities of heaven placed over us? What do you think about it? Do you think we plighted our faith and came here with that view and under that covenant? And, in this respect, is the whole world on the same footing?...

Did we covenant to be subject to the authority of God in all the different relations of life—that we would be loyal to the legitimate powers that emanate from God? I have been led to think that such is the truth. Something whispers these things to me in this light....[4]

What did we agree to before we came here? If to anything, I suppose the very same things we agreed to since we did come here, that are legitimate and proper. The husband agreed to be a faithful servant of God, to do his duty to all that were placed under his charge. The wife, on her part, covenants that she will be a faithful and devoted wife, and will obey her husband in the Lord in all things. If this were so, it is all right; for it is just as we are taught on the earth. [5]

Our Earthly Circumstances Are Related to Our Pre-Mortal Existence

As explained in Chapter 6 of this book, some of the spirit children of our Father in Heaven progressed further in pre-mortality than did others and were therefore "elected and foreordained" to receive certain blessings and to perform certain works when in mortality.

In addition to being "elected and foreordained" it also appears from modern scripture and prophetic discourses that if not all then at least some of the pre-mortal spirit children of our Heavenly Father had in varying degrees the opportunity and right to determine with our Eternal Father when, where, how, and under exactly what circumstances they would enter into mortality and dwell upon this earth. In regard to this fact of our entering mortality under previously earned and chosen circumstances, in 1922 Elder Melvin J. Ballard, an apostle, said the following:

Now, my brothers and sisters, I would like you to understand that long before we were born into this earth we were tested and tried in our pre-existence and the fact that of the thousands of children born today, a certain proportion of them went to the Hottentots of South Africa, thousands went to the Chinese mothers, thousands to Negro mothers, thousands to beautiful white Latter-day Saint mothers. Why this difference, you cannot tell me that the entire group was just designated, marked, to go where they did. That they were men and women of equal worthiness. There are no infant spirits born. They had a being ages before they come into this life. They appear in infant bodies, but they were tested, proven souls. *Therefore, I say to you that long before we came into this life all groups and races of men existed as they exist today. Like attracts to like.*

Why is it in this Church we do not grant the priesthood to the Negroes? It is alleged that the Prophet Joseph said—

and I have no reason to dispute it—that it is because of some act committed by them before they came into this life.... I am convinced it is because of some things they did before they came into this life that they have been denied the privilege. The races of today are very largely reaping the consequence of a previous life.*

That is why the Lord in giving Daniel the interpretation of that wonderful dream of Nebuchadnezzar was able to tell very clearly, long before they were born, when the various people should rise and bear rule upon the earth. There was a group of tested, tried and proven souls before they were born into the world, and the Lord provided a lineage for them. That lineage is the House of Israel, the lineage of Abraham, Isaac and Jacob and their posterity. Through this lineage were to come the true and tried souls that had demonstrated their righteousness in the spirit world before they came here. We came through that lineage. Our particular branch is the House of Joseph through his son Ephraim. That is the group from whence shall come the majority of the candidates for celestial glory. That is why we are doing the work for our ancestors and not for others.

In addition, Elder Duane S. Crowther, a noted Latter-day Saint author and publisher, has expertly summarized in the following discourse a few of our most important earthly circumstances that are a direct result of the type of life we magnified during pre-mortality:

There is evidence that some pre-mortal spirits are able to choose their mortal parents and are able to request parentage who will be suitable to the level of activity they have decided to pursue. Apostle Orson Hyde taught that some pre-mortal spirits have been able to choose the family into which they are to be born, and have sought their own level here on earth:

"So, when those spirits come to take bodies, where will the noble and high order of them go? *Will they take bodies that have come through a low and degraded parentage? No, no more than the righteous man will take up his abode with the vile and wicked.* Where will he go? 'Why,' says that noble spirit, that is swelling with light and intelligence, 'I will take a body through an honorable parentage; *I will have a body*

* Negroes are now permitted to receive priesthood ordination. This change was made by a revelation to the Church in June, 1978. For further information on the subject, see the author's book "His Servants Speak."

that will correspond with my mind; I will go to the place where purity and righteousness dwell.'

"Where do the spirits of a lower grade go? Among the lowest, and uncultivated, where the cultivation of the principles of virtue and integrity is in part or entirely neglected. In this way the sins of the fathers are answered upon their children to the third and fourth generation.

"Do good spirits want to partake of the sins of the low and degraded? No; but they will stay in heaven until a way is opened for purity and righteousness to form a channel in which they can come, and take honorable bodies in this world, and to magnify their calling."

An experience of Edward James Wood while president of the Canadian Temple lends weight to the teaching that some children are allowed to choose their parents before coming to earth:

"Several of the couples of the mission had been married for years and had never been blessed with children. I admonished them to join in this great movement [excursion to the temple] and they would receive the blessing they had hoped for and prayed for. Two such couples were with the caravan. In one of the sessions in the temple, President Wood *saw two spirits hovering over the congregation. He told all present that they were from the Spirit World and were anxious to come to the earth and take mortal bodies.* He promised the sisters in the room who had come for that special blessing would have their hearts' desires granted. *All had the experience of witnessing spirits from the unseen world come and stand in their very presence and even the angel's choir sang with joy.* In less than one year from that date, those two homes were blessed with babies."

Additional evidence that children are not sent to earth by happenstance but are designated to be born into particular families is found in the spirit world experience of Henry Zollinger, who during the eight hours he was separated from his body, was taken from the spirit world area he had entered to another portion of God's creation:

"My guide then took me and showed me *the spirits of the children that would yet come to my family* if we would be faithful. *They were full grown but not in the same sphere as those which had lived upon this earth."*

Other choices concerning mortal life were apparently available to the spirit children of the Father also. There is indication that pre-mortal spirits were allowed to choose the type of trials and hardships they would have to endure while on the earth. Consider the experience of Niels P. L. Eskildz, a Danish convert to the Church, who was seriously crippled and deformed when but ten years of age. The sixteen years which followed were a time of misery and despair for him. However, in the summer of 1862, just prior to his baptism, he received a revelation which helped him to understand many of the unexplained circumstances of his earth life:

"While engaged preparing his evening meal a glorious vision burst upon his view. It was not a single scene that he beheld, but a series of them.... He beheld as with his natural sight, but he realized afterwards that it was with the eye of the spirit that he saw what he did. His understanding was appealed to as well as his sight. What was shown him related to his existence in the spirit world, mortal experience and future rewards. He comprehended, as if by intuition, that *he had witnessed a somewhat similar scene in his pre-mortal state, and been given the opportunity of choosing the class of reward he would like to attain to. He knew that he had deliberately made his choice. He realized which of the rewards he had selected, and understood that such a reward was only to be gained by mortal suffering*—that, in fact, he must be a cripple and endure severe physical pain, privation and ignominy. *He was conscious too that he still insisted upon having that reward, and accepted and agreed to the conditions.*

"He emerged from the vision with a settled conviction, that *to rebel against or even to repine at his fate, was not only a reproach to an Alwise Father whose care had been over him notwithstanding his seeming abandonment, but a base violation of the deliberate promise and agreement he had entered into, and upon the observance of which his future reward depended.*"

Elder John Taylor was another who believed that spirits in their pre-mortal state were able to affect the course of their mortal life by means of choices and covenants which they made in the pre-existence. As he explained the past, present, and future status of faithful Latter-day Saint women he taught that in addition to some being able to choose their parents, some pre-mortal spirits were permitted to covenant with others to be their spouse, their children, and their guardian angel. His statement effectively summarizes the teachings of the others cited in this section:

"Knowest thou not that eternities ago *thy spirit, pure and holy, dwelt in thy Heavenly Father's bosom, and in His presence, and with thy mother, one of the queens of heaven, surrounded by thy brother and sister spirits in the spirit world, among the Gods?* That as thy spirit beheld the scenes transpiring there, and thou grewest in intelligence, thou sawest worlds upon worlds organized and peopled with thy kindred spirits who took upon them tabernacles, died, were resurrected, and received their exaltation on the redeemed worlds they once dwelt upon. Thou being willing and anxious to imitate them, waiting and desirous to obtain a body, a resurrection and exaltation also, and *having obtained permission, madest a covenant with one of thy kindred spirits to be thy guardian angel while in mortality, also with two others, male and female spirits, that thou wouldst come and take a tabernacle through their lineage, and become one of their offspring. You also chose a kindred spirit whom you loved in the spirit world* (and who had permission to come to this planet and take a tabernacle), *to be your head, stay, husband and protector on the earth and to exalt you in eternal worlds. All these were arranged, likewise the spirits that should tabernacle through your lineage.* Thou longed, thou sighed and thou prayed to thy Father in heaven for the time to arrive when thou couldst come to this earth, which had fled and fallen from where it was first organized, near the planet Kolob. Leaving thy father and mother's bosom and all thy kindred spirits thou camest to earth, took a tabernacle, and imitated the deeds of those who had been exalted before you.

"At length the time arrived, and thou heard the voice of thy Father saying, go daughter to yonder lower world, and take upon thee a tabernacle, and work out thy probation with fear and trembling and rise to exaltation. But daughter, remember you go on this condition, that is, you are to forget all things you ever saw, or knew to be transacted in the spirit world; you are not to know or remember anything concerning the same that you have beheld transpire here; but you must go and become one of the most helpless of all beings that I have created, while in your infancy, subject to sickness, pain, tears, mourning, sorrow and death. But when truth shall touch the cords of your heart they will vibrate; then intelligence shall illuminate your mind, and shed its lustre in your soul, and you shall begin to understand the things you once knew, but which had gone from you; you shall then begin to understand and know the object of your creation. Daughter, go, and be faithful as thou has been in thy first estate.

"Thy spirit, filled with joy and thanksgiving, rejoiced in thy Father, and rendered praise to His holy name, and the spirit world resounded in anthems of praise to the Father of spirits. Thou bade father, mother and all farewell, and *along with thy guardian angel, thou came on this terraqueous globe. The spirits thou hadst chosen to come and tabernacle through their lineage, and your head having left the spirit world some years previous,* thou came a spirit pure and holy. Thou hast obeyed the truth, and *thy guardian angel ministers unto thee and watches over thee. Thou hast chosen him you loved in the spirit world to be thy companion.* Now crowns, thrones, exaltations and dominions are in reserve for thee in the eternal worlds, and the way is opened for thee to return back into the presence of thy Heavenly Father, if thou wilt only abide by and walk in a celestial law, fulfill the designs of thy Creator and hold out to the end that when mortality is laid in the tomb, you may go down to your grave in peace, arise in glory, and receive your everlasting reward in the resurrection of the just, along with thy head and husband. *Thou wilt be permitted to pass by the Gods and angels who guard the gates, and onward, upward to thy exaltation in a celestial world among the Gods."*

If an individual, while in the form of a pre-mortal spirit, has been able to choose his parents and relatives, then has he elected the time and general location of his birth and life activity? If he has been privileged to choose the nature of his mortal probation and the challenges which he must overcome, has he also chosen the length of his probation, and hence the time of his death?....

Although man does not fully understand how the time of his death is fixed, yet it is clear that mortals have such a time set for them. The author of Ecclesiastes taught that man has "a time to be born, and a time to die." A significant passage concerning the healing of the sick, found in the Doctrine and Covenants, also speaks of the set time of death of an individual:

"It shall come to pass that he that hath faith in me to be healed, and *is not appointed unto death,* shall be healed."

The righteous man, who gives due care to his physical being and fulfills his obligations to the Lord, may expect the privilege of remaining on earth to fulfill his life's mission and course and living the full extent of his appointed years. The Savior, for example, went unharmed in several situations where he suffered bodily attack because "his hour was not yet come." But when his mission approached its culmination on the cross he then told his apostles, "The hour is come, that the Son of man should be glorified."

A servant of the Lord may expect divine protection so that he may complete his authorized mission from the Lord and not be slain before his time. The prophet Abinadi was able to withstand the murderous advances of the wicked priests of King Noah with the warning,

"Touch me not, for God shall smite you if ye lay your hands upon me, for I have not delivered the message which the Lord sent me to deliver,...therefore, *God will not suffer that I shall be destroyed at this time.*"

His warning was strengthened by the "exceeding luster" with which his face shone, and his assailants shrunk back in fright. Yet after his mission was completed the protection ceased and Abinadi was martyred by fire.

In the Doctrine and Covenants we read of the Lord's promise to Lyman Wight that

"I will bear him up as on eagles' wings; and he shall beget glory and honor to himself and unto my name.

"That *when he shall finish his work I may receive him unto myself....*"

The deathbed blessing of Joseph Smith, Sr. upon the head of his son, Joseph the prophet, was a promise that his life would be preserved until his life's mission was completed:

" 'Joseph, my son, you are called to a high and holy calling. You are even called to do the work of the Lord. Hold out faithful and you shall be blest and your children after you. *You shall even live to finish your work.'* At this Joseph cried out, weeping, 'Oh! my father, shall I?' 'Yes,' said his father, *'you shall live to lay out the plan of all the work which God has given you to do.* This is my dying blessing upon your head in the name of Jesus. I also confirm your former blessing upon your head; for it shall be fulfilled. Even so. Amen.'

This promise was fulfilled, and Joseph's life was preserved until after he completed his mission and placed the responsibility for guiding the Church on the shoulders of the Twelve.

Appointed Time of Death Changed by Pleas of the Righteous

There is evidence that the fixed time of death is not unalterable and that a number of factors can occasion a change in one's appointed death date. Apparently the requests of the righteous may prevail with the Lord to gain an extension of life in some instances....[7]

Our Pre-Mortal Characteristics Are Brought With Us Into Mortality

Just as some of our circumstances in this world are related to the type of life we magnified in our pre-mortal existence so is the individual character we now possess somewhat a product of the "light and truth" we acquired in pre-mortality. Concerning this fact within the gospel, the Church has published the following:

The extent of influence brought to bear on us in mortality by our premortal characteristics, is not yet clear. We will undoubtedly understand it at some time in the future. However, we do have some knowledge about this matter.

First, some of the premortal spirits were denied mortal bodies, while others were given them. This was explained to Abraham on the basis of the support or opposition which these spirits gave to the Gospel plan of salvation. (Abraham 3:26, 28.) Our choice in this matter had the most important effect for all of us.

Second, some were made leaders in mortality and given various responsibilities because of the qualities they had demonstrated before birth. Jeremiah was told of this (Jeremiah 1:5), and Abraham was shown that this was true of himself and many others. (Abraham 3:22, 23.)

Third, our places in the House of Israel or elsewhere were probably determined by previous behavior, as was also our time of coming to the earth, in many instances. (Acts 17:22-26; Deuteronomy 32:7-9.) Elder Ezra Taft Benson gave expression to such a thought as follows:

...It is my conviction that the finest group of young people that this world has ever known anything about has been born under the covenant into the homes of Latter-day Saint parents. I have a feeling that in many cases, at least, these choice spirits have been held back to come forth in this day and age when the Gospel is upon the earth in its fulness, and that they have great responsibilities in establishing the kingdom.

Fourth, influences may unquestionably be brought to bear on our mortal minds through the medium of our premortal spirits in an effort to help us make the most of our lives here. The Prophet Joseph Smith spoke of this in one of his last sermons in Nauvoo.

All things whatsoever God of his infinite wisdom has seen fit and proper to reveal to us while we are dwelling in mortality, in regard to our mortal bodies, are revealed to us in the abstract and independent of affinity of the mortal tabernacle; but are revealed to our spirits precisely as though we had no bodies at all; and those revelations which will save our spirits will save our bodies. God reveals them to us in view of no eternal dissolution of the body, or tabernacle.

We may suppose that the ability of our spirits to comprehend God's revelations and to influence the mortal behavior of their earthly entities is affected by the light and truth or intelligence possessed by the spirits themselves. Hence, if this be true, our present lives may be more favorably influenced if we faithfully acquired light and truth before mortality, than if we were less diligent at that time.

It is a matter of interest to know as much as we can about our premortal life and how it has affected us here. It is much more important, however, to learn this one lesson from those facts—that the quality of our lives at any one time will reach ahead and influence what we shall attain in the future. Those who keep their various estates, be it the first or second, by acquiring light and truth, by developing nobility and devotion to truth, and by spending their time and energy in vigorous promotion of God's purposes among men, will be added upon throughout their endless lives. The proof of this fact lies all about us and may be read in every human life. In this thing, everyone may know, if he will but see. We need not rest on the level of faith. It is as Browning says, however, for some do not see; and "...only he who sees takes off his shoes." [8]

In addition, another Church article similarly states:

Unto Abraham the Lord said that Abraham was one of those in the premortal life who was "good," and, therefore, he was selected as a "ruler"—"chosen before thou wast born." (Abr. 3:22-23.) This fact is an example of what we observe in this life—the differences among people as to intelligence, dispositions, and talents. Are these differences to be considered as having their origin in the earth-life? The answer is found in a number of discussions by Latter-day Saint authorities who have considered that the earth-life is but a continuation of the life before this one, and that there is a carry-over from the former existence. Elder James E. Talmage said:

"Every spirit born in the flesh is an individual character, and brings to the body prepared for its tenancy a nature all its own. The tendencies, likes and dislikes, in short the whole disposition of the spirit may be intensified or changed by the course of mortal life, and the spirit may advance or retrograde while allied with its mortal tabernacle....

"The spirit lived as an organized intelligence before it became the embodied child of human parents; and its pre-existent individualism will be of effect in its period of earth life. Even though the manifestations of primeval personality be largely smothered under the tendencies due to bodily and prenatal influence, it is there, and makes its mark." (*The Vitality of Mormonism* [Boston: Gorham Press, 1948], p. 232.)[9]

Physical Deformities in Mortality Are Not the Result of Pre-Mortal Punishment

Although it appears that spirits in pre-mortality are aware of the circumstances and choice they have of coming into this earth life with a body possibly possessing physical deformities,[10] yet, it must be understood that physical defects at birth are "due to some accident or other cause that can be laid at the door of mortal conditions" and are not related "to some pre-mortal defect or punishment" in the pre-earthly spirit world.[11] In regard to this subject and conclusion President Joseph Fielding Smith has said the following:

> The Lord revealed to the Prophet Joseph Smith the following:
> "Every spirit of man was innocent in the beginning; and God having redeemed man from the fall, men became again... innocent before God.
> "And that wicked one cometh and taketh away light and truth, through disobedience, from the children of men, and because of the tradition of their fathers." (D & C 93:38-39.)
> We must in all reason conclude that some physical defect at birth is due to some accident or other cause that can be laid at the door of mortal conditions and not to some premortal defect or punishment in the spirit world. When the disciples came to the Savior and asked the question concerning the man who was born blind, the question whether this defect came upon him because of a condition existing in the spirit world, he gave them the assurance that such was not the case. We have reason to believe that every spirit that comes into this world was whole and free from such defects in the pre-existence.
> Morality is subject to far different laws from those which exist in the world of spirits, evidently. The defects at birth must be considered to be due to misfortunate conditions prevailing in this mortal world. We came here in a world that is subject to mortal conditions. Sickness, disease, deformities, and such must be considered to be misfortunate conditions which are confined to the imperfect conditions in mortality. It does not seem to be consistent with heavenly conditions for defects of a physical nature, which evidently belong to the body, not the spirit, to be existing in the spirit world.
> We are definitely taught in the scriptures that we, the children of this world, are the offspring of God. This is taught us in the scriptures. Here are two passages that are accepted by all Latter-day Saints covering this point. One is in the vision given to the Prophet Joseph Smith and Sidney Rigdon, February 16, 1832, when they were taught that the children of men are spiritually "begotten sons and daughters of

God." (*Ibid.*, 76:24.) The other is in the prophetic utterance of the Apostle Paul as he stood on Mars' hill teaching the Greeks, before the altar with the inscription: *"To the unknown God."* Evidently these Greeks had before them a statement that we are the "offspring" of God. Therefore Paul in his discourse called their attention to this correct statement and then argued in behalf of the proper worship of the Supreme Being, calling their attention to the fact that even in their national belief they were ignorantly worshipping the Divine Creator, and he said to them:

"God that made the world and all things therein, seeing that he is Lord of heaven and earth, dwelleth not in temples made with hands;

"Neither is worshipped with men's hands, as though he needed any thing, seeing he giveth to all life, and breath, and all things;

"And hath made of one blood all nations of men for to dwell on all the face of the earth, and hath determined the times before appointed, and the bounds of their habitation;

"That they should seek the Lord, if haply they might feel after him, and find him, though he be not far from every one of us:

"For in him we live, and move, and have our being; as certain also of your own poets have said, For we are also his offspring.

"Forasmuch then as we are the offspring of God, we ought not to think that the Godhead is like unto gold, or silver, or stone, graven by art and man's device." (Acts 17:24-29.)

This idea that people could be deformed, blind, or otherwise maimed before they were born, it seems, was believed in ancient times.

However, it is a ridiculous notion that the spiritual offspring of God would be subject to spiritual defects before they were born into mortality. We are subject to all the vicissitudes that go with a temporal existence, sickness and physical defects as well as health, but such things will not exist in the world of spirits nor in the kingdom of God after the resurrection. The Lord has made this perfectly clear.[12]

CHAPTER TEN

The Creation of the Earth

Our Father in Heaven, Jesus Christ, and Michael, Begin the Creation of the Earth

As mentioned in Chapter 7 of this book, sometime during our pre-mortal existence as spirit children of our Father in Heaven an "organization" or "Council of Gods," in which our Father in Heaven and Jesus Christ were probably included, came together to plan for the arrangement, creation, and peopling of this earth and of others.

Following the decisions of the "Council of Gods" relevant to the creation of this world and the subsequent great "Council" and "War in Heaven," much activity was undertaken by our Father in Heaven, our Savior, Michael the Archangel (Adam), and other "great and noble" spirit children of our Eternal Father to prepare this earth for its eventual habitation by mortal man.[1] In regard to the creation of our earth by our Father in Heaven, Jesus Christ, and Michael, President Brigham Young has said the following:

> It is true that the earth was organized by three distinct characters, namely, Eloheim, Jehovah, and Michael, these three forming a quorum, as in all heavenly bodies, and in organizing element....[2]

The Earth is Organized First Spiritually, then Physically

In discussing the actual organization or creation of our earth, which first took place spiritually and then later physically, this author wishes to quote the following intensively written discourse by Elder W. Cleon Skousen, who has expertly presented the creation of our earth as it is taught in the light of modern scripture and revelation. This author hopes that the reader will follow Elder Skousen's written discourse, which is entitled "A Working Memorandum On The Creation Story," with an inquiring mind and perceptive spirit so that a proper understanding of our earth's actual creation may be gained:

The Lord told Moses that He was temporarily restricting some aspects of the Creation story (Moses 1:35), but promised that the full story would be told at the beginning of the Millennium (D&C 101:32-34).

Note that the Lord told Moses that "only an account of THIS earth, and the inhabitants thereof, give I unto you," and then the Lord appears to have further restricted the information concerning even this earth where it involved relationships with other earths. We have therefore come to realize that the Creation story was deliberately left obscure in some respects.

Nevertheless, it would seem quite obvious that the Lord never intended that what he DID reveal should become obscure.

By the time of Joseph Smith the Bible account was being twisted and manipulated to provide the basis for teaching all kinds of notions concerning the Creation. Even the text had been changed. The Lord therefore restored the account so that today we have the Creation story the way Moses originally wrote it. Later, we obtained the account given by Abraham.

This, of course, automatically opened up the whole subject of the Creation to a new study based on the additional information which the Lord had placed in our hands. This study is a continuing task. That is why I have called this paper a "Working Memorandum."

At the start, perhaps I should mention that it has always seemed to this writer that one of the greatest contributions which came with the restored text of Genesis was the explanation as to why there are *two* Creation stories in the Bible. As Joseph Smith pointed out in D&C 77:2, the first creation was spiritual, the second temporal. Scholars had thought the two stories in Genesis 1 and Genesis 2 were actually different versions of the same events. They acknowledged, however, that there were serious contradictions between the two accounts. For example in Genesis 1, man is created on the sixth day and is the *last* of God's creations. In Genesis 2, man comes *first*. And he and all the creations come on the *seventh* day!

It was a tremendous breakthrough to learn that Genesis 1 was the spiritual creation and the Church leaders began pointing this out. Both Orson Pratt and B. H. Roberts wrote or spoke extensively on the subject, as we shall see later. In a sermon to the studentbody of Brigham Young University, President Hugh B. Brown entitled a talk "What is Man and What He May Become." He said, "The information given in the scriptures on the time involved in the first great acts of creation, refers *only to the spiritual creation.*"(Italics added.) When Joseph Fielding Smith was writing his brochure on the *Origin of the Reorganized Church,* he made specific reference to the creation of man in Genesis 1:29-30 and after quoting these verses said, "This was a *spiritual creation,* man was created in the image of God, male and female, *first in the spirit,* and told in that *spiritual creation* that they were expected to multiply and replenish the earth when they were placed upon it. This we prove from the second chapter of Genesis beginning with the fifth verse:

"For I, the Lord God, created all things of which I have spoken (referring to Genesis 1) *spiritually* before they were naturally upon the face of the earth; for I, the Lord God, had not caused it to rain upon the face of the earth.

"And I, the Lord God, had created all the children of men, and not yet a man to till the ground, for in heaven created I them, and there was not yet flesh upon the earth, neither in the water, neither in the air."

The above quotation appears on page 99 of the *Origin of the Reorganized Church* with italics added. This represents the traditional position of the Church leaders concerning Genesis 1 being the basic scripture on the spiritual creation.

It is interesting that the Temple service follows the creation story in Moses 2 (the restored text of Genesis 1) rather than the creation pattern set forth by Abraham. In other words, it follows the spiritual creation until it is time to place man on the temporal earth and then shifts down to the temporal earth without the slightest hint as to how *it* was prepared for habitation.

As we shall see later, it is Abraham who emphasizes the *temporal* creation. He does not give us any detail as to *how* it was prepared but sets forth the *order* in which the preparation took place. In his presentation man does not come to the earth until the *seventh* day so this clearly identifies it with the temporal creation (see D & C 77:22).

In fact, if we let Genesis 1 tell the story of the spiritual creation and let Abraham 4 tell the story of the temporal creation we suddenly discover an apparent harmonizing of everything that both scripture and Church leaders have thus far disclosed concerning the Creation epic.

Let us now examine *both* creation stories verse by verse. The scope of this presentation may be more easily grasped by first going through it in terms of the topical headings. The citations and commentary may then be digested at the reader's leisure.

Genesis, Chapter One, Which (According to
B. H. Roberts, Orson Pratt, and Others)
Describes the Creation of the "Spirit" World.

The text is taken from the Inspired Version of Genesis, Ch. 1. See the Book of Moses, Pearl of Great Price, Ch. 2. In other words, this is Genesis, Chapter 1, the way Moses originally wrote it.

Account of the Creation Dictated to Moses
by Direct Revelation From God.

And now, Moses, my son, I will speak unto thee concerning this earth upon which thou standest; and *thou shalt write* the things which I shall speak. (Moses 1:40)

Moses Knew Creation Story Would Be Mutilated
and Have to Be Restored.

And in a day when the children of men shall esteem my words as naught and take many of them from the book which thou shalt write, behold, I will raise up another like unto thee; and they shall be had again among the children of men—among as many as shall believe. (Moses 1:41)

Creation Story Begins. Only Begotten [Jesus Christ]
of the Father in Charge of the Work.

And it came to pass that the Lord spake unto Moses, saying: Behold, I reveal unto you concerning this heaven, and this earth; write the words which I speak. I am the Beginning and the End, the Almighty God; by mine Only Begotten I created these things; yea, in the beginning I created the heaven, and earth upon which thou standest. (Moses 2:1)

Earth Without Form and Void. Spirit of God Moves
Across the Waters.

And the earth was without form, and void; and I caused darkness to come up upon the face of the deep; and my Spirit moved upon the face of the water; for I am God. (Moses 2:2)

The First Day. Let There Be Light.
Light Divided From the Darkness.

And I, God, said: Let there be light; and there was light. And I, God, saw the light; and that light was good. And I, God, divided the light from the darkness.

And I, God, called the light Day; and the darkness, I called Night; and this I did by the word of my power, and it was done as I spake; and the evening and the morning were the first day. (Moses 2:3-5)

The Second Day. The Waters Are Divided in Two Parts
With a Firmament Between.

And again, I, God, said: Let there be a firmament in the midst of the water, and it was so, even as I spake; and I said: Let it divide the waters from the waters; and it was done;

And I, God, made the firmament and divided the waters, yea, the great waters under the firmament from the waters which were above the firmament, and it was so even as I spoke.

And I, God, called the firmament Heaven; and the evening and the morning were the second day. (Moses 2:6-8)

The Third Day. Dry Land Appears. Grass, Herbs and
Fruit Trees Established.

And I, God, said: Let the waters under the heaven be gathered together unto one place, and it was so; and I, God, said: Let there be dry land; and it was so.

And I, God, called the dry land Earth; and the gathering together of the waters, called I the Sea; and I, God, saw that all things which I had made were good.

And I, God, said: Let the earth bring forth grass, the herb yielding seed, the fruit tree yielding fruit, after his kind, and the tree yielding fruit, whose seed should be in itself upon the earth, and it was so even as I spake.

And the earth brought forth grass, every herb yielding seed after his kind, and the tree yielding fruit, whose seed should be in itself, after his kind; and I, God, saw that all things which I had made were good.

And the evening and the morning were the third day. (Moses 2:9-13)

The Fourth Day. Earth Assigned Its Place Among
the Stellar Bodies.

And I, God, said: Let there be lights in the firmament of the heaven, to divide the day from the night, and let them be for signs, and for seasons, for days, and for years.

And let them be for lights in the firmament of the heaven to give light upon the earth; and it was so.

And I, God, made two great lights; the greater light to rule the day, and the lesser light to rule the night, and the greater light was the sun, and the lesser light was the moon; and the stars also were made even according to my word.

And I, God, set them in the firmament of the heaven to give light upon the earth.

And the sun to rule over the day, and the moon to rule over the night, and to divide the light from the darkness; and I, God, saw that all things which I had made were good;

And the evening and the morning were the fourth day. (Moses 2:14-19)

The Fifth Day. Fish and Aquatic Creatures Introduced.
  Birds and Fowl Fill the Air.

And I, God, said: Let the waters bring forth abundantly the moving creature that hath life, and the fowl which may fly above the earth in the open firmament of heaven.

And I, God, created great whales, and every living creature that moveth, which the waters brought forth abundantly, after their kind; and I, God, saw that all things which I had created were good.

And I, God, blessed them, saying: Be fruitful, and multiply and fill the waters in the sea and let fowl multiply in the earth;

And the even and the morning were the fifth day. (Moses 2:20-23)

The Sixth Day. Animals Introduced. Man Created
  in God's Image, Male and Female

And I, God, said: Let the earth bring forth the living creature after his kind, cattle, and creeping things, and beasts of the earth after their kind, and it was so;

And I, God, made the beasts of the earth after their kind, and everything which creepeth upon the earth after his kind; and I, God, saw that all these things were good.

And I, God, said unto mine Only Begotten, which was with me from the beginning: Let us make man in our image, after our likeness; and it was so. And I, God, said: Let them have dominion over the fishes of the sea, and over the fowl of the air, and over the cattle, and over all the earth, and over every creeping thing that creepeth upon the earth.

And I, God, created man in mine own image, in the image of mine Only Begotten created I him; male and female created I them.

And I, God, blessed them, and said unto them: Be fruitful, and multiply, and replenish the earth, and subdue it, and have dominion over the fish of the sea, and over the fowl of the air, and over every living thing that moveth upon the earth.

And I, God, said unto man: Behold, I have given you every herb bearing seed, which is upon the face of all the earth, and every tree in the which shall be the fruit of a tree yielding seed; to you it shall be for meat.

And to every beast of the earth, and to every fowl of the air, and to everything that creepeth upon the earth, wherein I grant life, there shall be given every clean herb for meat; and it was so, even as I spake.

And I, God, saw everything that I had made, and, behold, all things which I had made were good; and the evening and the morning were the sixth day. (Moses 2:20-31)

The Seventh Day. This Creation Finished. God Rests.
All Things Pronounced Good.

Thus the heaven and the earth were finished, and *all the host of them.*

And on the seventh day I, God, ended my work, and all things which I had made; and I rested on the seventh day from all my work, and all things which I had made were finished, and I, God, saw that they were good;

And I, God, blessed the seventh day, and sanctified it; because that in it I had rested from all my work which I, God, had created and made. (Moses 3:1-3)

God Verifies That All of the Foregoing Pertains to the
Spiritual Creation

And now, behold, I say unto you, *these* are the generations of the heaven and of the earth, when they were created, in the day that I, the Lord God, made the heaven and the earth;

And every plant of the field *before* it was in the earth, and every herb of the field *before it grew.* For I, the Lord God, create *all things, of which I have spoken, spiritually,* before they were naturally upon the face of the earth. For I, the Lord God had not caused it to rain upon the face of the earth. And I, the Lord God, had created *all the children of men:* and not yet a man to till the ground; *for in heaven created I them;* and there was *not yet flesh upon the earth,* neither in the water, neither in the air.... (Moses 3:4-5)

Compiler's Note:

Now notice what the Lord has said thus far. He has told us about the creation of a planet which was set in its proper place among the cosmic bodies of the universe. On that sphere plants, fish, birds, animals and human beings were brought forth until there was a "host" of them. Finally, the whole creative process was completed and God rested.

Then, to our amazement, we are told that the creation story just related to us is not talking about the physical planet of the earth upon which we are now residing. Instead, it is talking about those generations of the heaven and the earth when God created everything "spiritually."

This would seem to clear up one of the most perplexing problems in the Bible. For centuries students have been puzzled by the contradictions which exist between the first two chapters of Genesis. Scholars engaged in the most painful intellectual girations trying to reconcile them. It was impossible. But now we learn, to our great relief, that these chapters are talking about two different things. The first chapter has reference to the spiritual creation and the second refers to the temporal planet where we now reside. Concerning this great contribution which came with the restoration of the Gospel, B. H. Roberts writes:

"Though we cannot understand the nature of this spiritual creation, yet to learn that the first account of the creation in the Bible is of a spiritual creation and the second of an actual or natural one, gives some comfort, from the fact that it removes all appearances of inconsistency or contradiction between the two accounts. For since they are descriptions of two different things instead of one thing, there is nothing in the law of consistency requiring the accounts of different events to be alike." (*The Gospel and Man's Relationship to Diety,* p. 277)

Orson Pratt, on November 12, 1879, gave practically a whole sermon on the new insight which came through modern revelation concerning the creation story. A small portion of that sermon is as follows:

"We used to read the first and second chapters of Genesis which give an account of the works of the Almighty, but did not distinguish between the spiritual work and the temporal work of Christ. Although there are some things in King James' translation that give us a little distinction between the two creations, yet we did not comprehend it....

But our Heavenly Father inspired his servant Joseph Smith, to translate several chapters more in the Book of Genesis, in December 1830, which gave a more full account, down to the days of the flood....

"We learn, therefore, when speaking of this spiritual creation, [in Gen. 1] that not only all the children of men, of all generations, and of all ages, were created spiritually in heaven, but that fish and fowls, and beast, and all animated things, having life, were first made spiritual in heaven, on the fifth and sixth days, before bodies of flesh were prepared for them on the earth; and that there was no flesh upon the earth until the morning of the seventh day. On that morning God made the first fleshly tabernacle and took man's spirit and put within it, and man became a living soul—the first flesh upon the earth—the first man also. Though it was the seventh day no flesh but this one tabernacle was yet formed. No fish, fowl and beast was as yet permitted to have a body of flesh. The second chapter of Genesis (new translation) informs us that the spirits of fowls were created in heaven, the spirits of fish and cattle, and all things that dwell upon the earth, had their pre-existence." (*J.D.*, Vol. 21, pp. 197-206)

Therefore, according to B. H. Roberts and Orson Pratt, the first chapter of Genesis is giving us a broad outline of the chronology of the creative processes during the pre-existence or spiritual stage and then the second chapter begins with the introduction of life down onto this present temporal planet which we now inhabit.

But wait! How did this temporal planet come into existence? Isn't the Lord going to tell us anything about the temporal creation of our present earth?

If Genesis were the only scripture available we certainly would be left in a quandry. Genesis does not begin speaking of this planet until it was ready for man some six thousand years ago. What happened before that?

Fortunately, we do have another wonderful scripture which gives us some help on this subject. This is the creation story given to the prophet, Abraham. This account deals with the *temporal* creation and follows a different pattern than the spiritual creation. The full text of Abraham's account is set forth in the following pages.

ABRAHAM'S ACCOUNT OF THE CREATION

Abraham Makes Only Passing Reference to the Spiritual Creation

Now the Lord had shown unto me, Abraham, the intelligences that were organized before the world was; and among all these were many of the noble and great ones;

And God saw these souls that they were good, and he stood in the midst of them, and he said: These I will make my rulers; for he stood among *those that were spirits,* and he saw that they were good; and he said unto me: Abraham, thou art one of them; thou wast chosen before thou wast born. (Abraham 3:22-23)

The Temporal Creation Preceded by a Planning Council in Heaven

And there stood one among them (the spirits) that was like unto God, and he said unto those who were with him: We will go down, for there is space there, and we will take of these materials, and we will make an earth whereon these may dwell:

And we will prove them herewith, to see if they will do all things whatsoever the Lord their God shall command them;

And they who keep their first estate shall be added upon; and they who keep not their first estate shall not have glory in the same kingdom with those who keep their first estate; and they who keep their second estate shall have glory added upon their heads for ever and ever.

And the Lord said: Whom shall I send? And one answered like unto the Son of Man: Here am I, send me. And another answered and said: Here am I, send me. And the Lord said: I will send the first.

And the second was angry, and kept not his first estate; and, at that day, many followed after him. (Abraham 3:24-28)

When Temporal Earth Was First Formed, It Was Empty and Desolate

And then the Lord said: Let us go down. And they went down at the beginning, and they, that is the Gods, organized and formed the heavens and the earth.

And the earth, after it was formed, was empty and desolate, because they had not formed anything but the earth; and darkness reigned upon the face of the deep, and the Spirit of the Gods was brooding upon the face of the waters.

The First Day. Let There Be Light. Light Divided
From Darkness.

And they (the Gods) said: Let there be light; and there was light.

And they (the Gods) comprehended the light, for it was bright; and they divided the light, or caused it to be divided from the darkness.

And the Gods called the light Day, and the darkness they called Night. And it came to pass that from the evening until morning they called night; and from the morning until the evening they called day; and this was the first, or the beginning, of that which they called day and night. (Abraham 4:3-5)

The Second Day. Water Above and Water Below
Divided by an Expanse

And the Gods also said: Let there be an expanse in the midst of the waters, and it shall divide the waters from the waters.

And the Gods ordered the expanse, so that it divided the waters which were under the expanse from the waters which were above the expanse; and it was so, even as they ordered.

And the Gods called the expanse, Heaven. And it came to pass that it was from evening until morning that they called night: and it came to pass that it was from morning until evening that they called day; and this was the second time that they called night and day. (Abraham 4:6-8)

The Third Day. Seas Gathered. Land Appears.
Temporal Earth Prepared to Accommodate Plant Life

And the Gods ordered, saying: Let the waters under the heaven be gathered together unto one place, and let the earth come up dry; and it was so as they ordered;

And the Gods pronounced the dry land, earth; and the gathering together of the waters, pronounced they, great waters; and the Gods saw that they were obeyed.

And the Gods said: Let us *prepare* the earth to bring forth grass; the herb yielding seed; the fruit tree yielding fruit, after his kind, whose seed in itself yieldeth its own likeness upon the earth; and it was so, even as they ordered.

And the Gods organized the earth to bring forth grass from its own seed, and the herb to bring forth herb from its own seed, yielding seed after his kind; and the earth to bring forth the tree from its own seed, yeilding fruit, whose seed could only bring forth the same in itself, after his kind; and the Gods saw that they were obeyed.

And it came to pass that they numbered the days; from the evening until the morning they called night; and it came to pass, from the morning until the evening they called day; and it was the third time. (Abraham 4:9-13)

The Fourth Day. Earth Assigned Its Place
in the Cosmic Universe

And the Gods organized the lights in the expanse of the heaven, and caused them to divide the day from the night; and organized them to be for signs and for seasons, and for days and for years;

And organized them to be for lights in the expanse of the heaven to give light upon the earth; and it was so.

And the Gods organized the two great lights, the greater light to rule the day, and the lesser light to rule the night; with the lesser light they set the stars also;

And the Gods set them in the expanse of the heavens, to give light upon the earth, and to rule over the day and over the night, and to cause to divide the light from the darkness.

And the Gods watched those things which they had ordered until they obeyed.

And it came to pass that it was from evening until morning that it was night; and it came to pass that it was morning until evening that it was day; and it was the fourth time. (Abraham 4:14-19)

The Fifth Day. Seas Prepared to Support Marine Life.
Preparations Also Made for Birds and Fowl

And the Gods said: Let us prepare the waters to bring forth abundantly the moving creatures that have life; and

the fowl, that they may fly above the earth in the open expanse of heaven.

And the Gods *prepared the* waters that they *might* bring
forth great whales, and every living creature that moveth,
which the waters were to bring forth abundantly after their
kind; and every winged fowl after their kind. And the Gods
saw that they *would* be obeyed, and that their *plan* was
good.

And the Gods said: We will bless them, and cause them
to be fruitful and multiply, and fill the waters in the seas or
great waters; and cause the fowl to multiply in the earth.

And it came to pass that it was from evening until
morning that they called night; and it came to pass that it
was from morning until evening that they called day; and it
was the fifth time. (Abraham 4:20-23)

The Sixth Time Or Day. Earth Prepared For
Animal Life. The Gods Plan To Bring Forth Man

And the Gods *prepared* the earth to bring forth the living
creature after his kind, cattle and creeping things, and
beasts of the earth after their kind; and it was so, as they
had said.

And the Gods organized the earth to bring forth the
beasts after their kind, and cattle after their kind, and every
thing that creepeth upon the earth after its kind: and the
Gods saw they would obey.

And the Gods took counsel among themselves and
said: Let us go down and form man in our image, after our
likeness; and we will give them dominion over the fish of the
sea, and over the fowl of the air, and over the cattle, and over
all the earth, and over every creeping thing that creepeth
upon the earth.

So the Gods went down to organize man in their own
image, in the image of the Gods to form they him, male and
female to form they them.

And the Gods said: We will bless them. And the Gods
said: We will cause them to be fruitful and multiply, and
replenish the earth, and subdue it, and to have dominion
over the fish of the sea, and over the fowl of the air, and over
every living thing that moveth upon the earth.

And the Gods said: Behold, we will give them every
herb bearing seed that shall come upon the face of all the

earth, and every tree which shall have fruit upon it; yea, the fruit of the tree yielding seed to them we will give it; it shall be for their meat.

And to every beast of the earth, and to every fowl of the air, and to everything that creepeth upon the earth, behold, we will give them life, and also we will give to them every green herb for meat, and all these things *shall* be thus organized.

And the Gods said: We will do everything that we have said, and organize them; and behold, they shall be very obedient. And it came to pass that it was from evening until morning they called night; and it came to pass that it was from morning until evening that they called day; and they numbered the sixth time. (Abraham 4:24-31)

Compiler's Note:

A careful reading of this Abraham text will disclose that the final *preparation* of the temporal earth was completed on the sixth day or "time." It is clear that when the Gods had finished on the sixth day and earth had been prepared and "organized" to the point where it would support human life. It had also been completely prepared so that it would support the advanced type of plant and animal life which were to make the earth a pleasant habitation for man. The Gods then counseled together as to the exact manner in which they would introduce man into the earth. They also talked about the plant and animal life which would be provided. The Gods then proceeded to go down on the sixth day (4:27) in anticipation of the great work they would do on the following day. Abraham makes it very clear (5:5) as does Moses (3:5) that the "prepared" earth was desolate at the end of the sixth day. There was no flesh upon it and no rain to support even plant life....[3]

Transplantation, Not Evolution, Is the Source of Life Upon This Earth

From the previous sub-chapter, this author will continue to quote Elder Cleon Skousen's written discourse on the creation of the earth and man's first introduction thereon. Hopefully the reader will gain from this part of Elder Skousen's work the truth that the first man, woman, and other living forms of life that now inhabit this world were originally "transplanted" by Deity from other planets to this one, and did not "evolve" through the falsehood of "organic evolution." Elder Skousen continues:

At this point the student cannot help pondering the exciting question, "*How* was the earth prepared so that it would support the higher types of life which presently exist upon the earth?" Were older and more primitive forms of life utilized over eons of time to lay down the strata of coal, the animal-produced lime deposits, the ingredients for oil and the development of a soil cover for the earth's crust?

And was the old life then catastrophically destroyed when the "preparation" was completed so that by the seventh day God could say with all accuracy that there was no rain, no plants, and no flesh upon the earth?

Orson Pratt makes allowances for just such a possibility in this sermon previously quoted. Here is the portion to this exact problem:

"In giving a history of the creation, he (the Lord) speaks of the formation of man out of the ground, how he took man's spirit that was created in heaven and put it within the body of man, and man became a living soul—the first flesh upon the earth, as recorded in the second chapter of Genesis. Now we have been in the habit of thinking that the various kinds of animals that have lived, according to geologists, were the first flesh on the earth, and we go away back millions of ages to see that these lower formations of life existed *before* man. But the Lord gives us different information from this. He shows us that among all the animated creatures of flesh, man was the first that was ever placed upon the earth *in this temporal condition,* contradicting the theories of geologists—that is, so far as placing man on the earth in this *present* probation is concerned. *What may have taken place millions of ages before the world was organized temporally for man to inhabit is not revealed;* but, so far as this *present* change is concerned, *that* took place about six thousand years ago, man was the first being that came upon the earth and inhabited a body of flesh and bones. Afterwards, (also) on the seventh day, out of the ground the Lord God created the beasts of the field. Go back to the first chapter of Genesis, and you will find that the beasts, etc., were formed on the *sixth* day or period, and that on the seventh day there was *no* flesh on the earth...." (Journal of Discourses, Vol. 21, p. 201, italics and emphasis added)[4]

Elder Orson Pratt has also said:

How many transformations this earth had before it received its present form of creation, I do not know. Geologists pretend to say that this earth must have existed many millions of years, and this assertion is generally made by men who do not believe in God or the Bible, to disprove the history of the creation of the world, as given by the Prophet Moses. We will go further than geologists dare to go, and say that the materials of which the earth is composed are eternal, they will never have an end....

How many transformations this earth passed through before the one spoken of by Moses, I do not know, neither do I particularly care. If it had gone through millions on millions of transformations, it is nothing to us. We are willing, for the sake of argument, to admit that the materials themselves are as old as geologists dare to say they are; but then, that does not destroy the idea of a God, that does not destroy the idea of a great Creator, who, according to certain fixed and unalterable laws, brought these materials, from time to time, into a certain organization, and then by his power completed the worlds that were thus made, by placing thereon intelligent and animated beings, capable of thinking and having an existence; and then again, for various reasons, he destroys their earthly existence, until finally he exalts them from their former condition, and makes them celestial in their nature.[5]

Note that Orson Pratt is perfectly willing to concede the possibility that ancient life may have inhabited the earth. Nevertheless, as he points out, the geologists are not correct in deducting that the ancient life is the ancestor of any life which is *now* on the earth. *It* was brought in new and fresh just a little over 6,000 years ago.

Brigham Young refers to this interplanetary transplant-ation of life and says "He (Adam) was the person who brought the animals and the seeds *from other planets* to this world." (Journal of Discourses, Vol. 3, p. 319.)

Actually, all that geology claims to have proven is the fact that ancient life started out very simply and was then followed by more complex forms. Not at any time have they been able to demonstrate that the simple life *produced* the more complex species. In fact, such a phenomenon would violate a very basic law of nature. Dr. Armin J. Hill, Dean of Physical and Engineering Sciences at BYU comments on this as follows:

"He (Darwin) theorized that life began with some comparatively simple form and 'evolved' into more complex forms, giving us all the different species, genera, and phyla which are known. This is a most dangerous kind of generalization for, while he had some good evidence that this principle could account for minor variations, he had no basis for assuming that it could account for major differences. Nevertheless, he, and those who followed him, worked assiduously to prove the general concept which came to be known as the theory of organic evolution. At first, considerable evidence piled up from a study of ancient fossil forms. These apparently could be arranged in quite a impressive 'ladder' up which, it was maintained, the form of life developed.... Those who accept the theory—for theory it still is—grasp desperately at any apparent support, yet quickly disregard any evidence which seems to be counter to it. This certainly is not a correct scientific attitude.

Let us see how well this theory that life evolved from comparatively simple forms agrees with other scientific knowledge. Darwin writes that 'man descended from lower forms.' This sentence has always puzzled me. Frankly, I cannot understand how something can descend from something lower than it is. The confusion in this sentence seems to convey the basic weakness of the whole idea. Logically we cannot have a descent from a lower form, and we shall shortly show that, if natural law only is involved, we cannot ascend from a lower form to a higher form without some outside assistance....

We have for nearly a hundred years been able to examine forms in terms of their relative complexities or levels of organization. We have also been able to study the various chemical and other natural transformations which can occur in terms of their effects upon the complexities of the systems which are transformed. We find in every known case where non-living processes are involved the transformation is in the direction which *decreases* the complexity of the system. *Never* in nature do we find a tendency for the complexity to increase of its own accord except, as I have said, in some—not all, by any means— of the processes related to (minor variations in) living forms. *This tendency for the complexity or degree of organization of a system to decrease whenever it undergoes a transforming process is so general that it is now known as the second law of thermodynamics.* It is considered as one of our most basic and general natural laws." (Letters to My Missionary Son, pp. 3-5)

Of course, within each specie of life there exists an amazing complex of potential variations which makes it possible for that specie to adapt itself to a changing environment. But the *specie* doesn't change. Even the most radical mutations still remain within the framework of the specie pattern. Scientific experiments to break the specie pattern have consistently failed. Commenting on this, Dr. Hill states:

"We have been experimenting with the fruit fly—*drosophila melano-gaster*—now for an equivalent of over thirty thousand years of human generations, using every known device to produce mutations. After all this, the experimenters have been forced to admit that though minor inheritable variations may have been produced, the offspring is still a fruit fly. Apparently we have here extensive proof that the scripture which says with regard to plant and animal life that 'each shall bear after its own kind' *is the statement of a fundamental law of nature.*" (See Moses 2:24-25)

Now that we have a bold hint from the modern prophets that the secret to the origin of life on earth is quite different than what men had imagined, we can look forward to the great revelation which God has promised in which he will fully disclose exactly how our earth was "prepared" for the modern life which now inhabits it.

God's Promise of a Revelation On How the Earth Was Made

In the Doctrine and Covenants, Section 101:32-34, the Lord makes this promise:

"Yea, verily I say unto you, in that day *when the Lord shall come,* he shall reveal all things—things which have passed, and hidden things *which no man knew,* things of the earth, *by which it was made,* and the purpose and the end ·thereof—things most precious, things that are above, and things that are beneath, things that *are in the earth, and upon the earth,* and in heaven."

Probably no one will appreciate this revelation more than the students of geology. Those who painfully and arduously tried to piece together the torn and broken seams of this ancient planet will find the true reward of their labors when the whole story is told by the Lord. Possibly there will be some aspects of the story which they successfully anticipated, and no doubt there will also be much which "no man knew." It will be sweet meat for the students of both science and scripture when the Lord tells just how he did it.

Now let us return to the scripture story of those few details which the Lord has already shared with us concerning the beginning of modern life on earth.

No Life On the Temporal Planet at the Beginning of the Seventh Day!

"For I, the Lord God, created all things, of which I have spoken, spiritually, before they were *naturally* upon the *face* of the earth. For I, the Lord God, had not caused it to rain upon the *face* of the (natural) earth. And I, the Lord God, had created *all* the children of men; and not yet a man to till the ground; for in heaven created I them; *and there was not yet flesh upon the* (natural) *earth, neither in the water, neither in the air.*" (Moses 3:5)

First Rain Comes to the "Prepared" Earth:

"But I, the Lord God, spake, and there went up a mist from the earth, and watered the whole face of the ground" Moses 3:6)

(Since the Lord stated in the previous verse that He had not "caused it to rain upon the face of the earth," it would clearly imply that not only was there *no flesh* but *no plant life* as well.)

Man Comes to Earth On the Seventh Day

First of all, we should remind ourselves that it was on the *seventh* day that man put in his appearance on this planet. Of course, in the spirit creation, man was brought forth on the *sixth day,* but it was on the *seventh* that he came into the temporal earth. The scripture says, "...God made the world in six days, and on the seventh day he finished his work, and sanctified it, and also *formed man out of the dust of the earth....*" (Doctrine And Covenants 77:12)

Man Placed On the Earth During the Seventh Day:

"And I, the Lord God, formed man from the dust of the ground, and breathed into his nostrils the breath of life; and man became a living soul, the *first flesh* upon the earth, the *first man* also; nevertheless, all things were before created; but spiritually were they created and made according to my word."

(In the material previously quoted from the words of Orson Pratt it was pointed out that Adam was the first flesh of all the flesh which is *now* upon the earth. Elder Pratt made allowances for the possibility that primitive creatures may have been used to *prepare* the earth but if so, it was extinct by the seventh day. New life had to be brought in from other planets and Adam was the *first* flesh to be brought in. Joseph Smith specifically stated that this occurred on the *seventh day*—D.C. 77:12.)

Brigham Young Says Adam Had Been Born of Parents On Another Earth

Brigham Young stated that "He (Adam) was made as you and I were made and no person was ever made on any other principle." In fact, the Lord told Moses what it meant to be "made from the dust of the earth." The Lord said it meant to be "*Born*...by water, and blood, and the spirit which I have made, and *so became of dust a living soul.*" (Moses 6:59)

Brigham Young stated that this was precisely the way Adam and Eve were made: "Adam was made from the dust of an earth, but not from the dust of *this* earth. He was made *as you and I were made* and no person was ever made on any other principle." (Journal of Discourses, Vol. 3:319)

He further stated: "Mankind are here because they are the offspring of parents (Adam and Eve) who were first brought here from another planet." (Discourses of Brigham Young, p. 160)

Brigham Young further stated that this knowledge was based on a revelation which he had personally received. (See Deseret News, Vol. 22, pp. 308-309 which reports the sermon of Brigham Young given in the Tabernacle June 8, 1873)

Keeping these facts in mind, let us now go back to
Moses and Abraham to complete the Creation story....

Garden of Eden Planted. Man Placed in it:

"And I, the Lord God, planted a garden eastward in
Eden, and there I put the man whom I had formed." (Moses
3:8)
(Everything in this and the following verse would imply
that plant life came *after* Adam.)

All Plants Have Spirits

"And out of the ground made I, the Lord God, to grow
every tree, naturally, that is pleasant to the sight of man. And
it became also a living soul. For it was *spiritual* in the day
that I created it...." (Moses 3:9)

Animals Also Have Spirits:

"And out of the ground I, the Lord God, formed every
beast of the field, and every fowl of the air; and commanded
that they should come unto Adam, to see what he would call
them; and they were *also living souls*; for I, God, breathed
into them the breath of life, and commanded that whatsoever
Adam called every living creature, that should be the name
thereof." (Moses 3:19)
(Commenting on the spiritual and temporal nature of all
creatures, Joseph Smith said: "...that which is temporal (is)
in the likeness of that which is spiritual; the spirit of man in
the likeness of his person, as also the spirit of the beast, and
every other creature which God has created." [D & C 77:2])

Adam Receives His Wife:

"...but as for Adam, there was not found an help meet
for him. And I, the Lord God, caused a deep sleep to fall
upon Adam; and he slept, and I took one of his ribs and
closed up the flesh in the stead thereof; And the rib which I,
the Lord God, had taken from man, made I a woman, and
brought her unto the man. And Adam said: This I know now
is bone of my bones, and flesh of my flesh; she shall be
called Woman, because she was taken out of man." (Moses
3:20-23)

*B. H. Roberts Comments on the Introduction
of Life Upon Our Present Planet:*

"As vegetation was created or made to grow upon some older earth, and the seeds thereof or the plants themselves were brought to our earth and made to grow, so likewise man and his help-meet were brought from some other world to our own, to people it with their children. And though it is said that the 'Lord God formed man from the dust of the ground'—it by no means follows that he was 'formed' as one might form a brick, or form the dust of this earth. We are all 'formed' of the dust of the ground, though instead of being molded as a brick we are brought forth by natural laws of procreation; so also was Adam and his wife in some older world. *And as for the story of the rib, under it I believe the mystery of procreation is hidden.*" (Man's Relationship to Deity, pp. 279-280).[6]

In conclusion, it is wise that all Latter-day Saints keep in mind the following words of the First Presidency relative to the Gospel truth that "Adam was 'the first man of all men'" upon this earth, and that "we are therefore in duty bound to regard him as the primal parent of our race:"

It is held by some that Adam was not the first man upon this earth, and that the original human being was a development from lower orders of the animal creation. These, however, are the theories of men. The word of the Lord declares that Adam was "the first man of all men" Moses 1:34), and we are therefore in duty bound to regard him as the primal parent of our race. It was shown to the brother of Jared that all men were created in the beginning after the image of God; and whether we take this to mean the spirit or the body, or both, it commits us to the same conclusion: Man began life as a human being, in the likeness of our Heavenly Father.

Joseph F. Smith
John R. Winder
Anthon H. Lund

The First Presidency
(1909)[7]

Christ Has Created Many Other Worlds Than Our Own

As we mentioned in Chapters five and ten of this book, in our pre-mortal existence Jesus Christ, under and through the direction of our Father in Heaven, became the Creator of this world and of other "worlds without number" (Moses 2:33, 35). The reasons as to why our Savior was rightfully able to act, while yet still a spirit in pre-mortality, as the creator of this world and of others has been explained by various Latter-day Saint students of the scriptures. Elder Orson Pratt has expressed:

God, through him (Jesus Christ), created...not only this little world, this speck of creation, but by him the worlds were made and created. How many we know not, for it has not been revealed. Suffice it to say, a great many worlds were created by him. Why by him? Because he had the birthright, he being the oldest of his father's family, and this birthright entitles him, not only to create worlds, but to become the redeemer of the inhabitants of this our earth, but of all the others whom he created by the will and power of his Father.[8]

And Elder Robert Millet has written:

"Jehovah, the pre-earth Christ, while speaking in the name of the Father (by divine investiture of authority), explained to Moses that "worlds without number have I created; and I also created them for mine own purpose; and *by the Son I created them, which is mine Only Begotten.* John the Beloved also spoke of Christ's powers before His (Christ's) entrance into mortality: "In the beginning was the Word, and the Word was with God, and *the Word was God.* The same was in the beginning with God. *All things were made by him:* and without him was not anything made that was made. He was in the world, and *the world was made by him,* and the world knew him not." The Apostle Paul gave a similar account of Christ's works when he spoke of the Master as having been "appointed heir of all things, *by whom he* (the Father) *made the* worlds." Finally, in this dispensation, Joseph Smith and Sidney Rigdon bore their testimonies of the living reality of Jesus, stating that "by him and through him, and of him, *the worlds are and were created....*One question that arises at this point concerns the evident nature of Jesus Christ's power before His birth on the earth; specifically, how did He exercise Godhood while yet in a spirit state? Elder Orson Pratt gave a beautiful explanation:

"Although Paul informs us that Jesus was called and made a High Priest centuries after the law was given, yet there is no doubt that *he was considered in the mind of his Father the same as a High Priest before the foundation of the world*; and that *by virtue of the Priesthood which he should, in a future age, receive, he could organize worlds and show forth almighty power.* God, by his foreknowledge, saw that his Son would keep all his commands, and determined, at a certain time, to call and consecrate him a High Priest; He determined, also that by virtue of that future consecration to the priesthood, he should, thousands of years beforehand, have power to create worlds and govern them, the same as if he had already received the consecration. All his marvelous acts and doings, therefore, prior to his consecration, were just as much the results of the authority of the Priesthood as those performed by him since that time." [9]

In regard to the number of worlds that our Savior has created under the direction of our Father in Heaven, Elder Melvin J. Ballard has written:

The Lord has created by and through His son, Jesus Christ, according to the Book of Moses, worlds without number, and numerous are they as the sands upon the seashore. In each one, undoubtedly, dwells a group of His children. Then how can He dwell in the presence of all these several groups at one and the same time? If you will read the 88th section of "Doctrine and Covenants," toward the latter part of that section the Lord undertakes to explain it.

The Lord told Joseph Smith how He looks upon these, His kingdoms, worlds without number, and He said, "I know them. I count them." And Moses wanted to know about them. But the Lord said unto Moses, "Only an account of this earth give I unto you."

There is something else to learn after we leave this earth, and I rejoice in the anticipation of further and greater knowledge concerning the things I do not now understand and comprehend. The Lord touched Joseph's understanding when He said: Behold, these are known to me. They are like a man having a field, and he sent a group of workers to this part of the field and gave them instructions what to do and told them he would visit them in their hour and in their time. He sent out the second group into another part of the field, and another group, and unto each of them he made the promise that he would visit them in their hour and in their time and season until they all would be made glad by the joy of his countenance. He would visit them from the first to the last and from the last to the first in one eternal round, each in his time, in his hour and in his season.

I presume that is the reason that the promise is made that Christ will dwell with men on this earth for a thousand years and that will be our day, our time and then I presume He will do as suggested in this 88th section, He will visit other places and kingdoms, but while absent from this group we will, nevertheless, be in His presence, in communication with Him.[10]

And as to the fact that we as pre-mortal spirit children of our Father in Heaven were witnesses to these various creations of our Eternal Father and Elder Brother Jesus Christ, Elder Robert Millet has additionally added:

For eons of time, glorified and perfected beings have been the means of bringing life, redemption, and exaltation to myriads of souls. The work of the Gods is to "bring to pass the immortality and eternal life of man," and it has been so forever. Long before our world came rolling into existence, billions of similar creations had passed away and risen to the state of celestial orbs. Undoubtedly we were allowed to witness much of the creation and ultimate glorification of earths like that of our own—we longed and sighed for the day to come when our state of progression would be such as to merit mortality. President John Taylor, while writing to the sisters of the Church, spoke in poetic language: "Knoweth thou not that eternities ago thy spirit, pure and holy, dwelt in thy Heavenly Father's bosom, and in His presence, and with thy mother, one of the queens of heaven, surrounded by thy brother and sister spirits in the spirit world, among the Gods? That as thy spirit beheld the scenes transpiring there, and thou grewest in intelligence, *thou sawest worlds upon worlds organized and peopled with thy kindred spirits who took upon them tabernacles, died, were resurrected, and received their exaltation on the redeemed worlds they once dwelt upon."* President Taylor then reminded the sisters that they had been extremely "willing and anxious to imitate them, waiting and desirous to obtain a body, a resurrection and exaltation also..."[11]

CHAPTER ELEVEN

The Veil of Mortal Forgetfulness

A Veil of Forgetfulness is Placed Upon Our Mortal Senses

Latter-day Saints acknowledge that we had an existence before being born into this world. However, it is very difficult for us to recall exactly what events transpired during our pre-mortal life as spirit children of our Father in Heaven or even as to how long we resided with Him before we came to this earth to inhabit bodies of flesh and blood.

The reason that we cannot remember the events of our pre-mortal existence is because our Eternal Father "has drawn a 'veil of forgetfullness' across our minds so that we cannot remember living with him." The main reason He has done this is so that we in mortality may "develop faith in Deity." [1]

Why Knowledge of Our Pre-Mortal Existence is Being Withheld From Us Now

Although the scriptures only mention the "'veil' of forgetfulness" in a few instances (Ether 3:6, 19), Elder Orson Pratt and President George Q. Cannon (who served as First Counselor in the First Presidency during the late 1800's) have given us considerable insight into why our Father in Heaven placed a "veil" across our minds here in mortality so that we could not remember "anything that transpired in our pre-existence." [2] Concerning this topic Elder Orson Pratt has said the following:

I know that the objection will immediately arise in the minds of individuals who have not reflected on this subject, if we were intelligent personages thousands of years ago, and dwelling in the presence of God, and of Jesus, our elder brother, how is it that we have no remembrance of anything that transpired in our pre-existence? I answer this question by saying, that when we came into this world from our former state of existence, and had our spirits enclosed within these mortal tabernacles, it had a tendency to take away our memories so far as the past was concerned. It did so in relation to Jesus. He had great knowledge before he was born into this world—sufficient to create the heavens and the earth, hence we read in the Hebrews that God, by his Son, made the worlds. This was before Jesus came here, and he must then have been the possessor of great knowledge to have been able to do that; but when he took upon himself flesh and bones did he forget this knowledge? We read in the Scriptures, speaking of Jesus coming here and taking a body of flesh and bones, that "in his humiliation his judgment was taken away." What humiliation? His descending from the presence of God his Father and descending below all things, his judgment was taken away, that is, his remembrance of things that were past, and that knowledge which, while in the presence of his Father, enabled him to make worlds, and he had to begin at the first principles of knowledge, just the same as all his brethren who came here in the flesh. We read that Jesus, as he grew in stature, grew also in wisdom and knowledge. If he had possessed all wisdom, and had not forgotten that which he formerly possessed, how was it that he could increase in wisdom as he increased in stature? It shows clearly that the wisdom which he had possessed thousands of years before, had for a wise purpose been taken from him. "His judgment was taken away" and he was left, as it were, in the very depth of humility, beginning at the very first principles of knowledge and growing up from grace to grace, as the Scriptures say, from one degree to another, until he received a fullness from his Father. Then when he did regain all his previous knowledge and wisdom, he had the fullness of the Father within him, in other words, "in him dwelt all the fullness of the Godhead bodily."

Now if his knowledge was forgotten, and his judgment taken away, why not ours? We find this to be the case. What person among all the human family can comprehend what took place in his first existence? No one, it is blotted from the memory, and I think there is great wisdom manifested in withholding the knowledge of our previous existence. Why? Because we could not, if we had all our pre-existent knowledge accompanying us into this world, show to our Father in the heavens and to the heavenly host that we would be in all things obedient; in other words, we could not be tried as the Lord designs to try us here in this state of existence, to qualify us for a higher state hereafter. In order to try the children of men, there must be a degree of knowledge withheld from them, for it would be no temptation to them if they could understand from the beginning the consequences of their acts, and the nature and results of this and that temptation. But in order that we may prove ourselves before the heavens obedient and faithful in all things, we have to begin at the very first principles of knowledge, and be tried from knowledge to knowledge, and from grace to grace, until, like our elder brother, we finally overcome and triumph over all our imperfections, and receive with him the same glory that he inherits, which glory he had before the world was.[3]

And President George Q. Cannon stated:

If we could understand the glory we once had with our Father in Heaven we would be discontented in dwelling in this condition of existence. We would pine for the home we left behind us. Its glory and its beauty, its heavenly graces and delights were of such a character that we would pine for it with that home-sickness that men have some partial knowledge of here on the earth. It is said that at one time in the French army, the bands were forbidden to play certain airs because of the effect they had upon the Swiss soldiers whom they employed. These Swiss airs would arouse such sensations of home sickness as to cause the Swiss to throw down their arms and desert and go back to their native valleys and mountains. Now, if such a feeling of home-sickness can be brought about in that way, how much more would it be the case if we could recollect our association with our Father and God in the eternal world! Wisely, in the providence of God, this knowledge is withdrawn from us. We can have a glimpse occasionally, through the revelations of the Spirit to us, of the glory there is awaiting us, and sometimes when men and women are approaching death—when they are ready to step out of this existence into the other—the veil becomes so thin that they behold the glories of the eternal world, and when they come back again—as some have, we all probably have met those who have been snatched from death—they come back to this mortal existence with a feeling of regret. They have had a foretaste of the glory that awaited them; they have had a glimpse of that glory that is behind the veil; and the love of life is so completely lost—the love of earthly home and friends so completely taken from them, that they desire with all their hearts to take their exit from this life into that glorious life which they knew was on the other side of the veil. Has not this been the case in many instances? Certainly it has. Therefore our God is His wisdom has withdrawn this knowledge from us, and left us to seek for and obtain that aid and strength necessary to enable us to successfully battle with and overcome the powers of evil that assail us on every hand.[4]

Our Remembrance of Our Pre-Mortal Existence Will Return To Us After Death

With the exception of the Savior and a few other prophets such as Adam, Moses, Enoch, the brother of Jared, and Joseph Smith,[5] the "veil of forgetfulness" about the pre-mortal existence remains with most of mankind throughout mortality. (For the accounts of some individuals who have been permitted while in mortality to see through the "veil" into the pre-mortal life, see Chapter 9 of this book.)

Regarding a time when the events of our pre-mortal existence will again come to our memory, Elder Orson Pratt has inferred that it may be after we have died and again "behold the face of our Father" in Heaven:

Now admit, as the Latter-day Saints do, that we had a previous existence, and that when we die we shall return to God and our former habitation, where we shall behold the face of our Father, and the question immediately arises, shall we have our memories so increased by the Spirit of the living God that we shall ever remember our previous existence? I think we shall. Jesus seems to have gained this even here in this world, otherwise he would not have prayed, saying, "Father, glorify thou me with that glory which I had with thee before the world was," showing plainly that he had obtained by revelation a knowledge from his Father of something about the glory that he had before the world was. This being the case with Jesus, why not his younger brethren also obtain this information by revelation? And when we do return back into the presence of our Father, will we not there also have our memories so quickened that we will remember his face, having dwelt in his presence for thousands of years? It will not be like going to visit strangers that we have never seen before. Is not this a comfort to persons who expect to depart from this life, like all the rest of the human family? They have a consolation that they are going not among strangers, not to a being whose face they never saw, but to one whom they will recognize, and will remember, having dwelt with him for ages before the world was....

These are the expectations of the Latter-day Saints: we do not expect to go among strangers. When we get back there we expect this place to be familiar to us, and when we meet this, that and the other one of all the human family that have been here on the earth, we shall recognize them as those with whom we have dwelt thousands of years in the presence of our Father and God. This renewing of old friendships and acquaintances, and again enjoying all the glory we once possessed, will be a great satisfaction to all who are privileged to do so. [6]

CHAPTER TWELVE

Adam and Eve As the First Man and Woman Upon the Earth

Adam and Eve Were Immortal Beings When First Placed in the Garden of Eden

As was explained in Chapter Ten of this book, Adam and Eve were born of parents after the same manner "as you and I were" and as youthful individuals were eventually "brought" to this earth by way of divine "transplantation...from another planet" and "placed in the Garden of Eden" as the first man and woman upon this earth.[1]

However, when Adam and Eve were first placed "on the earth," they were not "mortal, like unto us." When they were initially placed in the Garden of Eden, Adam and Eve were immortal beings" not "subject to any kind of pain," affliction, or death.[2]

Regarding this fact of the Gospel, Elder Orson Pratt has said the following about the initial immortal state of Adam and Eve:

Now, perhaps those who are not in the habit of reflecting upon this matter, may suppose that when Adam was placed on the earth, and Eve, his wife, they were mortal, like unto us; but that was not so. God did not make a mortal being. It would be contrary to this great goodness to make a man mortal, subject to pain, subject to sickness, subject to death. When he made this creation, and when he made these two intelligent beings and placed them upon this creation, he made them after his own likeness and his own image. He did not make them mortal, but he made them immortal, like unto himself. If he had made them mortal, and subject to pain, there would have been some cause, among intelligent beings, to say that the Lord subjected man, without a cause, to afflictions, sorrows, death and mortality. But he could not do this; it was contrary to the nature of his attributes, contrary to the nature of that infinite goodness which dwells in the bosom of the Father and the Son, to make a being subject to any kind of pain. At the time of the creation, all things that proceeded forth from his hands were considered very good. How came, then, Adam to be mortal? How came Adam to be filled with pain and affliction and with great sorrow? It was in consequence of transgression. Hence, the Apostle Paul, in speaking upon this subject, said, that by transgression sin entered into the world, and death by sin. Death, then, instead of being something that the Lord created, instead of being something that he sent into the world, and by sin; the Lord suffered it to come upon Adam in consequence of transgression. Two immortal beings, then, were placed in the garden of Eden, male and female.[3]

And similar to what Elder Pratt has previously said, President Brigham Young has stated that Adam (and therefore Eve) came "into the garden of Eden" with an immortal "celestial body" which did not become mortal until after they "had eaten of the forbidden fruit."

Now hear it, O inhabitants of the earth, Jew and Gentile, Saint and sinner! When our father Adam came into the garden of Eden, he came into it with a celestial body, and brought Eve, one of his wives, with him. He helped to make and organize this world. He is Michael, the Archangel, the Ancient of Days! about whom holy men have written and spoke.... When Adam and Eve had eaten of the forbidden fruit, their bodies became mortal from its effects, and therefore their offspring were mortal.[4]

The Location of the Earth When Adam and Eve First Inhabited It

When Adam and Eve were first placed upon our earth as immortal beings, the earth was not located in its present position within our galaxy. Instead, "prior to the fall" of Adam and Eve from immortality to mortality the earth was located near the great star Kolob, which apparently is a very large celestial star located "near unto the throne" of our Father in Heaven.[5] Concerning this subject, Elder Cleon Skousen has written and illustrated the following details:

The Earth Originally Organized Near Kolob:

In his writings President John Taylor refers to "this earth which had fled and fallen from where it was *organized near... Kolob.*" (Quoted by N. B. Lundwall, *The Vision,* p. 146.)

Brigham Young taught the same doctrine. (See N. B. Lundwall, *Assorted Gems,* p. 346; also see *J.D.,* Vol. 3, p. 319.)

The Earth Operated on Kolob's Time Prior to the Fall:

"Now I, Abraham saw that it was after the Lord's time, which was after the time of Kolob; for as yet the Gods had not appointed unto Adam his reckoning." (Abraham 5:13)

"And the Lord said unto me, by the Urim and Thummim, that Kolob was after the manner of the Lord, according to its times and seasons in the revolutions thereof; that *one revolution* was a *day* unto the Lord, after his manner of reckoning, it being *one thousand years* according to the time appointed unto that whereon thou standest. This is the reckoning of the Lord's time, according to the reckoning of Kolob." (Abraham 3:4)

(This would clearly imply that prior to the Fall, the earth was rotating only once in every thousand years instead of every 24 hours!)

Abraham Shown the Present Location of our Solar System— Nearly 2/3 of the Way Out From the Center of Our Galaxy

"And I saw the stars, that they were very great, and that one of them was nearest unto the throne of God; and there were many great ones which were near unto it;

"And the Lord said unto me: These are the governing ones; and the name of the great one is Kolob, because it is near unto me, for I am the Lord thy God; I have set this one (Kolob) to govern all those which belong to the same order as that upon which thou standest." (Abraham 3:2-3)

(Note that if Kolob is only *one* of the governing stars near unto the throne of God and each of the governing stars is the center of a Galaxy, then the residence of the Father is surrounded by *many* galaxies, not just ours.)

"And the Lord said unto me: Now, Abraham,...it is given unto thee to *know the times of reckoning,* and the set time, yea, the set time of the earth upon which thou standest, and the set time of the greater light which is set to rule the day, and the set time of the lesser light which is set to rule the night.... And thus there shall be the reckoning of the time of one planet above another, until thou come nigh unto Kolob, which Kolob is after the reckoning of the Lord's time; which Kolob is set nigh unto the throne of God, to govern all those planets which belong to the same order as that upon which thou standest. *And it is given unto thee to know the set time of all the stars that are set to give light, until thou come near unto the throne of God."* (Abraham 3:6-10)

(In Joseph Smith's interpretation of facsimile #2 we find a list of planets and stars which seem to be lined up as indicated below.)[6]

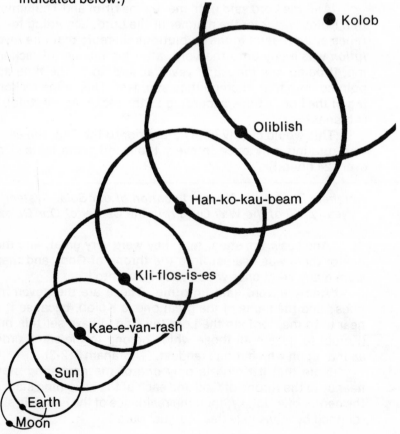

The Marriage of Adam and Eve Was Performed by the Lord

Although there presently appears to be no information available as to exactly when or where Adam and Eve were married, nevertheless, we do know that sometime prior to their knowing "anything about death"[7] Adam and Eve were personally united "as husband and wife" by our "Lord" (probably referring to our Savior Jesus Christ)[8] through the holy covenant of eternal marriage (Moses 3:21-25).[9] Regarding this subject, Elder Orson Pratt has stated his belief:

> Do you enquire what was the form of that first marriage between Adam and Eve? I will explain it in a few words. They were united as husband and wife by the Lord himself; when they were united they did not know anything about death, for they had not partaken of the fruit of the tree that was forbidden, and they were then immortal beings. Here were two beings united who were as immortal as you will be when you come forth from your graves in the morning of the first resurrection. Under these conditions Adam and Eve were married.[10]

The Two Commandments Given to Adam and Eve When They Were Still Immortal

When Adam and Eve, as immortal beings, were first placed upon this earth in the "Garden of Eden," which was located somewhere on the American Continent,[11] our Lord God gave unto them two important commandments. The first and foremost commandment our Lord God gave unto our "first parents" was "that they be fruitful, and multiply, and replenish the earth, and subdue it." The second commandment was that "they refrain from eating or even touching the fruit of a certain tree, the tree of knowledge of good and evil, which grew in the midst of the garden; though of all other fruits they were at liberty to freely partake."[12] Of these two commandments given by God to our "first parents" the scriptures state:

> And I, God, created man in mine own image, in the image of mine Only Begotten created I him; male and female created I them.
> And I, God, blessed them, and said unto them: Be fruitful and multiply, and replenish the earth, and subdue it, and

have dominion over the fish of the sea, and over the fowl of the air, and over every living thing that moveth upon the earth.[13]

And:

And I, the Lord God, commanded the man, saying: Of every tree of the garden thou mayest freely eat,

But of the tree of the knowledge of good and evil, thou shalt not eat of it, nevertheless, thou mayest choose for thyself, for it is given unto thee; but, remember that I forbid it, for in the day thou eatest thereof thou shalt surely die.[14]

CHAPTER THIRTEEN

The Transition of Adam and Eve from Immortality to Mortality

The Fall of Adam and Eve Into Mortality

As immortal beings upon this earth Adam and Eve greatly enjoyed living within the "Garden of Eden," which their Creator had made into a very "choice region of the earth" and had "embellished...with natural beauties to gladden the heart of its" first inhabitants.[1]

However, this state of blissful existence which Adam and Eve enjoyed for some duration was soon to be interrupted by the "arch enemy" of all truth and righteousness—the evil and rebellious spirit—Satan![2]

Because his diabolical plan of "forced redemption" had been rejected by God and the righteous spirits present during the premortal grand "Council in Heaven," Satan and "a third part of the hosts of heaven," who later joined him in his rebellion against God were eventually "cast down" to the earth as spirit entities—without the hope of ever gaining mortal bodies.[3] Because these evil spirits recognized that without a mortal body and supremacy over the power of God they would be doomed to a state of eternal "non-progressive existence," they sought to destroy what they thought was the intended designs, plans, and workings of God—hopeful that they could ultimately succeed in overthrowing our Father in Heaven, His power, and His works.[4]

Therefore, when the first opportunity presented itself for the possible temptation of Adam or Eve to disobey one of the commandments that the Lord God had previously given them, Satan "entered into a beast, called a serpent" and tempted Eve in the Garden of Eden, and that was the beginning of his power on this earth."[5] (See Moses 4:4-26.)

145

In regard to the temptation which Satan advanced towards Eve and the events which transpired thereafter, which have become known as the "Fall of Adam and Eve" from immortality into mortality,[6] Elder J. Preston Creer has expertly written the following discourse:

The hour of temptation soon came. Lucifer, who had so lately been consigned to the regions of anguish and woe, again waged war against the righteousness of Jehovah. Cunningly, he laid his plans to foil the purposes of the Almighty, and wittingly did he, with specious argument, deceive the weaker of Eden's occupants. To Eve he made his appearance, and, in phrases most pleasing, persuaded her to eat of the fruit of the tree of knowledge of good and evil, saying: "For God doth know that in the day ye eat thereof, then your eyes shall be opened, and ye shall be as gods, knowing good and evil." Seeing that the tree was beautiful, and the words of Satan delightful, the woman plucked and ate of the forbidden fruit whose mortal taste brought death with all its woes into the world. Adam learning of what had been done, and remembering the two commandments of God, studied well his peculiar position. Being honest and faithful, he desired to obey the will of his Father, but under existing circumstances, this was impossible. Eve, having disobeyed God, became mortal, and could no longer enjoy the pleasurable companionship of her husband. This Adam knew, and undoubtedly he argued: how can the first and great commandment be fulfilled unless I break the second? So with a knowledge of the attendant consequences, he chose to follow his wife, and eat. Of this disobedience Paul says, "Adam was not deceived, but the woman being deceived was in the transgression...."

The fall opened the eyes of our first parents, and they now discerned between good and evil. For the first time, they beheld their own nakedness, and made garments... [to cover their nakedness]. Soon the voice of Jehovah was heard, and in reply the feeble words of Adam, "Here I am," broke upon the ear of his Creator. Calmly, the Father spoke unto the woman saying: "I will greatly multiply thy sorrow and thy conception, in sorrow thou shalt bring forth children, and thy desire shall be unto thy husband, and he shall rule over thee"; while unto the man he said: "Because thou hast hearkened unto the voice of thy wife, and hast eaten of the tree of which I commanded thee saying, Thou shalt not eat of it, cursed is the ground for thy sake, in sorrow shalt thou eat of it all the days of thy life. Thorns also and thistles shall it bring forth to thee, and thou shalt eat the herb of the field. In the sweat of thy face shalt thou eat bread till thou return unto the ground."

In order that Adam and Eve might not partake of the fruit of the tree of life and live forever, being as gods, knowing good and evil, they were expelled from the garden and Cherubim with a flaming sword was stationed to guard the gate.

What a radical change our first parents must have been constrained to endure. One day living in paradise, surrounded with all the grandeur that divine art could display, feeling no pain, sorrow, nor regret, ignorant of the frailties of mortality, and rocked in the cradle of universal peace; the next, living amidst the hills and dales of mother earth; sheltered by the blue canopy of heaven; encircled by dreary plains and barren bluffs; tasting of the pangs incident to this probation, and sensing most keenly the follies of the flesh. Fear now invaded the field of hope, while anxiety strolled the path of contentment. And all this was done not to satisfy the exigencies of chance, but to fulfill the purposes of a most benign Father, that in his glory, he might be sustained and upheld by the undying loyalty of an exalted, glorified, and immortalized family.[7]

In perhaps more detail as to why Adam chose to partake of the "forbidden fruit" once Eve had informed him that she had done so, Elder Orson Pratt has said the following:

Adam very well knew that his wife, Eve, after she had partaken of the forbidden fruit, having transgressed the law of God, must die. He knew this; he knew that she would have to be cast out of the garden of Eden, from the presence of her husband; she could no longer be permitted to dwell with him. Hence, inasmuch as there was a great separation threatened between husband and wife—the wife having transgressed—he concluded that he would not be separated from the woman, and hence he was not deceived, but the woman was deceived; he partook of the forbidden fruit to prevent a separation between the two, and fell, even as the woman fell, and both were cast out together. If one only had

transgressed and been cast out, the great command that had
been given prior to that time—to multiply and replenish the
earth—could not have been fulfilled, because of the separation. In order, therefore, that the command first given might
be fulfilled, Adam, though not deceived, partook of the forbidden fruit, was cast out with Eve, and hence began, as far
as possible, to fulfil the command, and to multiply his
species upon this earth.[8]

When Adam and Eve fell from immortality into mortality,
the "earth" likewise "fell" from its celestial location near the star,
Kolob, which was "near unto the throne of God," out to its present location within our solar system.[9]
Because of this totally physical change with both Adam and
Eve now possessing bodies of flesh and blood and the earth now
situated in a new heavenly location and orbit, the "effects" of
" 'the fall' of our first parents" is presently felt by us all.[10] Concerning the effects that Adam and Eve's transgression had upon
them, and consequently upon us, as their posterity, Elder James
E. Talmage has concluded with the following written summaries:

> *The Immediate Result of the Fall was the substitution of
> mortality,* with all its attendant frailties, for the vigor of the
> primeval deathless state. Adam felt directly the effects of
> transgression in finding a barren and dreary earth, with a
> relatively sterile soil, instead of the beauty and fruitfulness
> of Eden. In place of pleasing and useful plants, thorns and
> thistles sprang up; and the man had to labor arduously,
> under the conditions of physical fatigue and suffering, to
> cultivate the soil that he might obtain necessary food. Upon
> Eve fell the penalty of bodily infirmity; pains and sorrows,
> which since have been regarded as the natural lot of woman-
> kind, came upon her, and she was made subject to her hus-
> band's authority. *Having lost their sense of former inno-
> cence they became ashamed of their nakedness and the
> Lord made for them garments of skins.* Upon both the man
> and the woman was visited the penalty of spiritual death;
> for in that very day they were banished from Eden and cast
> out from the presence of the Lord. The serpent, having
> served the purposes of Satan, was made a subject of divine
> displeasure, being doomed to crawl forever in the dust, and
> to suffer from the enmity which it was decreed should be
> placed in the hearts of Eve's children.

Atonement Provided for—God did not leave His now mortal children without hope. *He gave other commandments to Adam, requiring him to offer sacrifices in the name of the Only Begotten Son,* and promising redemption unto him and all his descendants who would comply with the conditions prescribed. The opportunity of winning the victor's reward by overcoming evil was explained to our parents, and they rejoiced. *Adam said: "Blessed be the name of God, for because of my transgression my eyes are opened, and in this life I shall have joy, and again in the flesh I shall see God."* Eve was glad and declared: "Were it not for our transgression we never should have had seed, and never should have known good and evil, and the joy of our redemption, and the eternal life which God giveth unto all the obedient."

The Fall Came Not by Chance—It would be unreasonable to suppose that the transgression of Eve and Adam came as a surprise to the Creator. By His infinite foreknowledge, God knew what would be the result of Satan's temptation to Eve, and what Adam would do under the resulting conditions. Further, it is evident that the fall was foreseen to be a means whereby man could be brought into direct experience with both good and evil, so that of his own agency he might elect the one or the other, and thus be prepared by the experiences of a mortal probation for the exaltation provided in the beneficent plan of his creation; *"For behold, this is my work and my glory—to bring to pass the immortality and eternal life of man"* spake the Lord unto Moses. It was the purpose of God to place within the reach of the spirits begotten by Him in the heavens the means of individual effort, and the opportunity of winning not merely redemption from death but also salvation and even exaltation, with the powers of eternal progression and increase. Hence it was necessary that the spiritual offspring of God should leave the scenes of their primeval childhood and enter the school of mortal experience, meeting, contending with, and overcoming evil, according to their several degrees of faith and strength. *Adam and Eve could never have been the parents of a mortal posterity had they not themselves become mortal;* mortality was an essential element in the divine plan respecting the earth and its appointed inhabitants; and, as a means of introducing mortality, the Lord placed before the progenitors of the race a law, knowing what would follow.

Eve was fulfilling the foreseen purposes of God by the part she took in the great drama of the fall; yet she did not partake of the forbidden fruit with that object in view, but with intent to act contrary to the divine command, being deceived by the sophistries of Satan, who also, for that matter, furthered the purposes of the Creator by tempting Eve; yet his design was to thwart the Lord's plan. We are definitely told that "he knew not the mind of God, wherefore he sought to destroy the world." Yet his diabolical effort, far from being the initiatory step toward destruction, contributed to the plan of man's eternal progression. Adam's part in the great event was essentially different from that of his wife; he was not deceived; on the contrary he deliberately decided to do as Eve desired, that he might carry out the purposes of his Maker with respect to the race of men, whose first patriarch he was ordained to be.

Even the transgressions of men may be turned to the accomplishment of high purposes. The sacrificial death of Christ was ordained from before the foundation of the world, yet Judas who betrayed, and the Jews who brought about the crucifixion of the Son of God, are none the less guilty of the awful crime.

It has become a common practice with mankind to heap reproaches upon the progenitors of the family, and to picture the supposedly blessed state in which we would be living but for the fall; whereas our first parents are entitled to our deepest gratitude for their legacy to posterity—the means of winning title to glory, exaltation, and eternal lives. But for the opportunity thus given, the spirits of God's offspring would have remained forever in a state of innocent childhood, sinless through no effort of their own; negatively saved, not from sin, but from the opportunity of meeting sin; incapable of winning the honors of victory because prevented from taking part in the conflict. As it is, they are heirs to the birthright of Adam's descendants—mortality, with its immeasurable possibilities and its God-given freedom of action. *From Father Adam we have inherited all the ills to which flesh is heir; but such are necessarily incident to a knowledge of good and evil, by the proper use of which knowledge man may become even as the Gods.*[11]

Adam and Eve as the Father and Mother of the Human Race

After the Lord God had "drove" Adam and Eve out of the Garden of Eden (Moses 4:31) and into a "barren and dreary earth," [12] our "first parents" began to keep the first commandment God had given them: that is to "multiply and replenish the earth" (Moses 2:28). As a consequence of their keeping this first commandment, all of us in mortality who have been born or ever will be born upon this earth are direct descendants of Adam and Eve.[13]

Although there is little information concerning the specific events which transpired in the lives of Adam and Eve after they were sent out of the Garden of Eden, we do know, however, that Adam and Eve were baptized "by the spirit of the Lord" (Moses 6:64-66), had a fulness of the gospel (Moses 5:57-59), and "begat many sons and daughters" in Adam's 930 years of mortal life (Moses 6:12). Of these prior events and a few others that occurred during the mortal lives of Adam and Eve the scriptures tell us the following:

> And it came to pass that after I, the Lord God, had driven them out, that Adam began to till the earth, and to have dominion over all the beasts of the field, and to eat his bread by the sweat of his brow, as I the Lord had commanded him. And Eve, also, his wife, did labor with him.
>
> And Adam knew his wife, and she bare unto him sons and daughters, and they began to multiply and to replenish the earth.
>
> And from that time forth, the sons and daughters of Adam began to divide two and two in the land, and to till the land, and to tend flocks, and they also begat sons and daughters.
>
> And Adam and Eve, his wife, called upon the name of the Lord, and they heard the voice of the Lord from the way toward the Garden of Eden, speaking unto them, and they saw him not; for they were shut out from his presence.
>
> And he gave unto them commandments, that they should worship the Lord their God, and should offer the firstlings of their flocks, for an offering unto the Lord. And Adam was obedient unto the commandments of the Lord.
>
> And after many days an angel of the Lord appeared unto Adam, saying: Why dost thou offer sacrifices unto the Lord? And Adam said unto him: I know not, save the Lord commanded me.
>
> And then the angel spake, saying: This thing is a similitude of the sacrifice of the Only Begotten of the Father, which is full of grace and truth.

Wherefore, thou shalt do all that thou doest in the name of the Son, and thou shalt repent and call upon God in the name of the Son forevermore.

And in that day the Holy Ghost fell upon Adam, which beareth record of the Father and the Son, saying: I am the Only Begotten of the Father from the beginning, henceforth and forever, that as thou hast fallen thou mayest be redeemed, and all mankind, even as many as will.

And in that day Adam blessed God and was filled, and began to prophesy concerning all the families of the earth, saying: Blessed be the name of God, for because of my transgression my eyes are opened, and in this life I shall have joy, and again in the flesh I shall see God.

And Eve, his wife, heard all these things and was glad, saying: Were it not for our transgression we never should have had seed, and never should have known good and evil, and the joy of our redemption, and the eternal life which God giveth unto all the obedient.

And Adam and Eve blessed the name of God, and they made all things known unto their sons and their daughters....

And it came to pass, when the Lord had spoken with Adam, our father, that Adam cried unto the Lord, and he was caught away by the Spirit of the Lord, and was carried down into the water, and was laid under the water, and was brought forth out of the water.

And thus he was baptized, and the Spirit of God descended upon him, and thus he was born of the Spirit, and became quickened in the inner man.

And he heard a voice out of heaven, saying: Thou art baptized with fire, and with the Holy Ghost. This is the record of the Father, and the Son, from henceforth and forever;

And thou art after the order of him who was without beginning of days or end of years, from all eternity to all eternity.

Behold, thou art one in me, a son of God; and thus may all become my sons....

And Adam and Eve, his wife, ceased not to call upon God. And Adam knew Eve his wife, and she conceived and bare Cain, and said: I have gotten a man from the Lord; wherefore he may not reject his words. But behold, Cain hearkened not, saying: Who is the Lord that I should know him?

And she again conceived and bare his brother, Abel. And Abel hearkened unto the voice of the Lord. And Abel was a keeper of sheep, but Cain was a tiller of the ground.

And Cain loved Satan more than God. And Satan commanded him, saying: Make an offering unto the Lord....

And it came to pass that Cain took one of his brothers' daughters to wife, and they loved Satan more than God.

And Satan said unto Cain: Swear unto me by thy throat, and if thou tell it thou shalt die; and swear thy brethren by their heads, and by the living God, that they tell it not; for if they tell it, they shall surely die; and this that thy father may not know it; and this day I will deliver thy brother Abel into thine hands.

And Satan sware unto Cain that he would do according to his commands. And all these things were done in secret.

And Cain said: Truly I am Mahan, the master of this great secret, that I may murder and get gain. Wherefore Cain was called Master Mahan, and he gloried in his wickedness.

And Cain went into the field, and Cain talked with Abel, his brother. And it came to pass that while they were in the field, Cain rose up against Abel, his brother, and slew him....

And the Lord said unto Cain: Where is Abel, thy brother? And he said: I know not. Am I my brother's keeper?

And the Lord said: What hast thou done? The voice of thy brother's blood cried unto me from the ground....

And Cain was shut out from the presence of the Lord, and with his wife and any of his brethren dwelt in the land of Nod, on the east of Eden....

And Adam hearkened unto the voice of God, and called upon his sons to repent.

And Adam knew his wife again, and she bare a son, and he called his name Seth. And Adam glorified the name of God; for he said: God hath appointed me another seed, instead of Abel, whom Cain slew.

And God revealed himself unto Seth, and he rebelled not, but offered an acceptable sacrifice, like unto his brother Abel. And to him also was born a son, and he called his name Enos.

And then began these men to call upon the name of the Lord, and the Lord blessed them;

And a book of remembrance was kept, in the which was recorded, in the language of Adam, for it was given unto as many as called upon God to write by the spirit of inspiration;

And by them their children were taught to read and write, having a language which was pure and undefiled....

And Adam lived one hundred and thirty years, and begat a son in his own likeness, after his own image, and called his name Seth.

And the days of Adam, after he had begotten Seth, were eight hundred years, and he begat many sons and daughters;

And all the days that Adam lived were nine hundred and thirty years, and he died....

(Moses, 5:1-12, 6:64-68, 5:16-18, 5:28-32, 5:34-35, 5:41, 6:1-6; 6:10-12)

Near the end of Adam and Eve's mortal lives, Adam, "as the presiding high priest (under Christ) over all the earth," called all of his righteous descendants together for a mighty conference. The conference was to be held at "Adam-ondi-Ahman," an area which today includes "the place now know as Spring Hill, Daviess County, Missouri."[14]

When all the righteous posterity of Adam had been gathered from throughout the various regions of the earth at "Adam-ondi-Ahman," Adam "blessed them with a patriarchal blessing...and foretold what should befall them to the latest generation."[15] Of this event Elder Bruce R. McConkie has written:

One of the greatest spiritual gatherings of all the ages took place in the Valley of Adam-ondi-Ahman some 5,000 years ago, and another gathering—of even greater importance relative to this earth's destiny—is soon to take place in that same location. Our revelations recite: "Three years previous to the death of Adam, he called Seth, Enos, Cainan, Mahalaleel, Jared, Enoch, and Methuselah, who were all high priests, with the residue of his posterity who were righteous, into the valley of Adam-ondi-Ahman, and there bestowed upon them his last blessing.

"And the Lord appeared unto them, and they rose up and blessed Adam, and called him Michael, the prince, the archangel. And the Lord administered comfort unto Adam, and said unto him: I have set thee to be at the head; a multitude of nations shall come of thee, and thou art a prince over them forever. And Adam stood up in the midst of the congregation; and, notwithstanding he was bowed down with age, being full of the Holy Ghost, predicted whatsoever should befall his posterity unto the latest generation." (D & C 107:53-56.)

At that great gathering Adam offered sacrifices on an altar built for the purpose. A remnant of that very altar remained on the spot down through the ages. On May 19, 1838, Joseph Smith and a number of his associates stood on the remainder of the pile of stones at a place called Spring Hill, Daviess County, Missouri. There the Prophet taught them that Adam again would visit in the Valley of Adam-ondi-Ahman, holding a great council as a prelude to the great and dreadful day of the Lord. (*Mediation and Atonement,* pp. 69-70.) At this council, all who have held keys of authority will give an accounting of their stewardship to Adam. Christ will then come, receive back the keys, and thus take one of the final steps preparatory to reigning personally upon the earth. (Dan. 7:9-14; *Teachings,* p. 157.)[16]

Adam and Eve Are Now Bringing Forth Immortal Sons and Daughters

Elder Orson Pratt once stated that it was his "belief" that Adam and Eve, after they had been resurrected at the time of Christ's resurrection,[17] came "forth and entered into celestial glory...and as immortal beings have brought forth immortal sons and daughters since their resurrection."[18] In reference to this "belief" Elder Pratt has said the following:

Was there any commandment given to those two immortal beings before the fall? There was one commandment, namely: "Be fruitful and multiply, and replenish the earth." What! Did the Lord command two immortal beings to multiply their species! He did. In meditating upon this great command given to these two immortal beings, it opens to us a field of reflection, of knowledge, concerning the great designs of the Almighty. It imparts to us a knowledge that the Lord our God intended that immortal beings should multiply their species. Can you find any place in the book of Genesis where our first parents were commanded to multiply after the fall? I do not remember any such scripture. I have read the scriptures very diligently; I do not remember any such command. Yet they did so, and the consequences were that children of mortality were born—mortal beings came upon the earth....

But will the time come in the endless duration of the future, when our first parents will fulfill that command which was given to them while they were yet children of immortality? In other words will the time ever come when Adam and Eve will become immortal and carry out the command that was given to them in the days of their first immortality? I answer, yes; without this, the command of God never could be, in all respects, fulfilled. Though there should be hundreds of thousands of millions, or more, of the descendants of those mortal beings come here upon the earth, the command is not fully complied with; though he may have begotten sons and daughters, Cain, Abel, Seth and many others for some nine hundred years and upwards, yet all the sons and daughters he begat while he was mortal here upon the earth did not, in all respects, fulfill the command given to him while an immortal being. That has to be fulfilled after Adam and Eve are resurrected from the grave. Have they yet been resurrected? I think so....

I have no doubt but what our first parents, Adam and Eve, were permitted to come forth and enter into celestial glory; and I have no doubt but what they have been fulfilling the commandment given to them before they fell. Nearly two thousand years have passed since the first resurrection of the Saints. I cannot believe that Adam and Eve, during these nineteen centuries, have been in idleness. I cannot believe that they alone constitute their whole family; but I believe that during this time they have been fulfilling literally the commandment that was given to them in the morn of creation, and as immortal beings have brought forth immortal sons and daughters since their resurrection. Thus the commandment of the Most High was not made void, but is in process of fulfillment.[19]

Thus it is that Adam and Eve have now attained to their exaltation and may now even be bringing forth "immortal sons and daughters," similar to what our Father in Heaven has done in the past and will continue to do forever.[20]

In conclusion, it is because Adam and Eve partook of the "forbidden fruit" that we are now here upon this earth experiencing mortality. However, in the final analysis it will be our own actions, diligence, and faithfulness while here in mortality, and not that of Adam and Eve, that will determine our place of residence and glory in the "mansions" of our Father in Heaven throughout the eternities which are to follow.[21]

Because of this fact, it is this author's hope and prayer that he and his family and all other of our Father's children now in mortality will "endure to the end" by striving to magnify their lives and callings that the Lord has given them while upon this earth and in the hereafter.

FOOTNOTES

Footnotes, Chapter One:

1. Gary Ellsworth, "Trailing Clouds of Glory," *The Ensign,* October, 1974, pp. 49-50.
2. Daniel H. Ludlow, "The Pre-Earthly Existence of Man," B.Y.U. Special Collections Article, November 3, 1957, p. 1.
3. William E. Berrett, "We Lived Before," B.Y.U. Speeches of the Year, November 12, 1957, p. 41.
4. Daniel H. Ludlow, "The Pre-Earthly Existence of Man," *op. cit.,* pp. 1-3.
5. Gary Ellsworth, "Trailing Clouds of Glory," *op. cit.,* pp. 49-51.
6. William E. Berrett, "We Lived Before," *op. cit.,* pp. 47-48.
7. "The Pre-Mortality of Mankind," *The Relief Society Magazine,* September, 1970, Vol. 57:707-708.
8. George Q. Cannon, *Journal of Discourses,* September 28, 1884, Vol. 26:184.
9. Harold B. Lee, "Understanding Who We Are Brings Self Respect," *The Ensign,* January, 1974, pp. 4-6.

Footnotes, Chapter Two:

1. Bruce R. McConkie, *Mormon Doctrine* (Bookcraft, Inc., Salt Lake City, Utah, 1966), pp. 387, 751.
2. Daniel H. Ludlow, "The Pre-Earthly Existence of Man," *op. cit.,* pp. 1-3. Elder Daniel Ludlow has additionally written that "the mind or the intelligence of man is essentially that part of your being with which you do your thinking." (*The Improvement Era,* January, 1962, pp. 17-18.) Joseph Smith, (*The Documentary*) *History of the Church* (Deseret Book Company, Salt Lake City, Utah, 1946-1951), Vol. 6:311.
3. Joseph Smith, (*History of the Church, op. cit.,*) quoted by Daniel H. Ludlow, *The Improvement Era,* January 1962, pp. 17-18.
4. Bruce R. McConkie, *Mormon Doctrine, op. cit.,* pp. 386-387.
5. D & C 93:29-30, 33-34; 131:7-8.
6. Daniel H. Ludlow, *The Improvement Era, op. cit.,* pp. 17-18.
7. Joseph Smith, "The King Follett Discourse," quoted by Gordon Allred, *Immortality* (Hawkes Publishers, Inc., Salt Lake City, Utah, 1974), pp. 62-63.

8. *Ibid.*

9. "Matter," *World Book Encyclopedia* (1975), pp. 246-247.

10. Joseph Fielding Smith, *The Progress of Man* (Genealogy Society, Salt Lake City, Utah, 1936), p. 11.

11. Orson Pratt, *The Millennial Star,* October 15, 1845, Vol. 6:157-159.

12. W. Cleon Skousen, "The Building Blocks of the Universe," (a non-classified article, of which a copy is presently in the possession of this author), pp. 1-6.

13. "The Pre-Mortality of Mankind," *The Relief Society Magazine,* September, 1970, pp. 705-706.

14. Daniel H. Ludlow, *The Improvement Era, op. cit.,* pp. 17-18.

15. Bruce R. McConkie, *Mormon Doctrine, op. cit.,* p. 750.

16. *Ibid.,* pp. 750-751.

17. William E. Berrett, "We Lived Before," *op. cit.,* pp. 43-44.

18. *Ibid.*

19. Sterling W. Sill, "Vision," B.Y.U. Speeches of the Year, September 25, 1954, pp. 5-6.

20. James E. Talmage, "Spirit and Matter, Without Beginning or End" (an open letter, B.Y.U. Library reference number: # Mor.— M230-Ala-284), p. 1.

21. *Ibid.*

Footnotes, Chapter Three:

1. Bruce R. McConkie, *Mormon Doctrine, op. cit., pp. 576-577.*

2. *Ibid., p. 577.*

3. *Ibid.*

4. *Ibid.*

5. W. Cleon Skousen, "The Building Blocks of the Universe," *op. cit.,* pp. 2-3.

6. *Ibid.*

7. Joseph Smith, *History of the Church, op. cit.,* Vol. 6:312-313.

8. Joseph Smith, "The King Follett Discourse," *op. cit.,* pp. 57-58.

9. Orson Pratt, *Journal of Discourses,* November 12, 1876, Vol. 18:292.

10. Bruce R. McConkie, *Mormon Doctrine, op. cit.,* p. 239.

11. *Ibid.,* pp. 317-318.

12. Orson Pratt, *Journal of Discourses,* November 12, 1876, Vol. 18:288.

13. Hyrum L. Andrus, "The Doctrine and Covenants and Man's Relationship to Deity," 37th B.Y.U. Leadership Week Lectures, June 4-9, 1960, Vol. 11, p. 5.

14. W. Cleon Skousen, "The Building Blocks of the Universe," *op. cit.,* pp. 11-13.

Footnotes, Chapter Four:

1. Brigham Young, *Journal of Discourses,* February 8, 1857, Vol. 4:215-216.
2. Orson Pratt (November 12, 1876), quoted in *The Mormon Doctrine of Deity,* by B. H. Roberts (Horizon Publishers, Bountiful, Utah, 1974), p. 270.
3. *Ibid.,* p. 260.
4. Bruce R. McConkie, *Mormon Doctrine, op. cit.,* pp. 750-751.
5. Orson Pratt (November 12, 1876), *The Mormon Doctrine of Deity, op. cit.,* p. 260.
   Orson Pratt, *Journal of Discourses,* December 15, 1872, Vol. 15:246.
6. Bruce R. McConkie, *Mormon Doctrine, op. cit.,* pp. 516-517.
7. Brigham Young, *Journal of Discourses,* February 8, 1857, Vol. 4:215-216.
8. *Ibid.,* April 9, 1852, Vol. 1:50.
9. *Ibid.,* March 8, 1857, Vol. 4:268.
10. Orson Pratt, *Journal of Discourses,* December 15, 1872, Vol. 15:246.
11. See Chapter 2 of this book.
12. Orson Pratt, *Journal of Discourses,* December 15, 1872, Vol. 15:242-243.
13. Sterling W. Sill, "Vision," *op. cit.,* p. 7.
14. Melvin J. Ballard, *The Three Degrees of Glory* (Deseret Book Company, Salt Lake City, Utah, September 22, 1922), pp. 10-11.
15. Daniel H. Ludlow, *The Improvement Era, op. cit.,* p. 17.
16. Lorenzo Snow, *Journal of Discourses,* 1872, Vol. 14:300,302.
17. Orson Pratt, *Journal of Discourses,* November 12, 1876, Vol. 18:293.

Footnotes, Chapter Five:

1. Bruce R. McConkie, *Mormon Doctrine, op. cit.,* p. 129.
2. "The Pre-Mortality of Mankind," *The Relief Society Magazine,* September, 1970, Vol. 57:703-704.
3. *Ibid.*
4. *Ibid.*
5. Brigham Young, *Journal of Discourses,* February 8, 1857, Vol. 4:215-216.
6. Gordon Allred, *Immortality, op. cit.,* pp. 58-60.
7. Bruce R. McConkie, *Mormon Doctrine, op. cit.,* p. 129.
8. Gordon Allred, *Immortality, op. cit.,* p. 64.

Footnotes, Chapter Six:

1. Orson Pratt, *Journal of Discourses,* (1876) Vol. 18:289-292; (1878) Vol. 20:75.

2. J. Preston Creer, "Fruits of the Fall," *The Improvement Era,* February, 1903, Vol. 6:276-279.
3. Orson Pratt, *Journal of Discourses,* November 12, 1876, Vol. 18:289-292.
4. *Ibid.,* August 25, 1878, Vol. 20:75.
5. Bruce R. McConkie, *Mormon Doctrine, op. cit.,* p. 590.
6. Charles H. White, "Pre-Existence," *The Improvement Era,* November, 1907, Vol. 2:27-31.
7. William E. Berrett, "We Lived Before," *op. cit.,* pp. 43-44.
8. Orson F. Whitney, "The Fall and the Redemption," *The Improvement Era,* March, 1921, Vol. 374-375.
9. "The Pre-Mortality of Mankind," *The Relief Society Magazine,* September, 1970, Vol. 57:705-706.
10. Robert L. Millet, *Magnifying Priesthood Power* (Horizon Publishers, Bountiful, Utah, 1974), pp. 41-43.
11. William E. Berrett, "We Lived Before," *op. cit.,* p. 45.
12. Robert L. Millet, *Magnifying Priesthood Power, op. cit.,* pp. 43-46.
13. "The Pre-Mortality of Mankind," *The Relief Society Magazine,* September, 1970, Vol. 57:706-707.

Footnotes, Chapter Seven:

1. Robert L. Millet, *Magnifying Priesthood Power, op. cit.,* pp. 38-39.
2. *Ibid.*
3. *Ibid.*
   Bruce R. McConkie, *Mormon Doctrine, op. cit.,* pp. 163-164.
4. James E. Talmage, *Jesus the Christ* (Deseret Book Company, Salt Lake City, Utah, 1961 ed.), p. 15.
5. Robert L. Millet, *Magnifying Priesthood Power, op. cit.,* p. 39.
6. *Ibid.*
7. Bruce R. McConkie, *Mormon Doctrine, op. cit.,* p. 164.
8. James E. Talmage, *Jesus the Christ, op. cit.,* p. 15.
9. *Ibid.*
   Bruce R. McConkie, *Mormon Doctrine, op. cit.,* p. 745.
10. Orson Pratt, *Journal of Discourses,* August 29, 1852, Vol. 1:55.
11. *Ibid.*
12. J. Preston Creer, "Fruits of the Fall," *op. cit.,* pp. 277-278.
13. Orson F. Whitney, "The Fall and the Redemption, *op. cit.,* p. 378.
14. James E. Talmage, *Jesus the Christ, op. cit.,* p. 15.
15. *Ibid.*
16. Bruce R. McConkie, *Mormon Doctrine, op. cit.,* p. 164.

17. *Pearl of Great Price,* Abraham 3:27.
18. *Ibid.*
19. *Pearl of Great Price,* Moses 4:2.
20. *Doctrine and Covenants,* 76:25-26; 93:25.
21. Bruce R. McConkie, *Mormon Doctrine, op. cit.,* pp. 164, 192-195.
    James E. Talmage, *Jesus the Christ, op. cit.,* p. 15.
22. Bruce R. McConkie, *Mormon Doctrine, op. cit.,* pp. 192-193.
23. Orson F. Whitney, "The Fall and the Redemption," *op. cit.,* p. 378.
24. James E. Talmage, *Jesus the Christ, op. cit.,* p. 15.
25. Orson Pratt, *Journal of Discourses,* November 22, 1873, Vol. 16:318.

Footnotes, Chapter Eight:

1. Bruce R. McConkie, *Mormon Doctrine, op. cit.,* pp. 618-619.
   R. Clayton Brough, "The War In Heaven" (a college paper prepared for a religion class at B.Y.U. The original copy of the paper is in the possession of this author), 1971, pp. 1-5.
2. *Pearl of Great Price,* Moses 4:4-5.
   Bruce R. McConkie, *Mormon Doctrine, op. cit.,* pp. 618-619.
3. Bruce R. McConkie, *Mormon Doctrine, op. cit.,* pp. 192-193.
4. J. Preston Creer, "Fruits of the Fall," *op. cit.,* Vol. 6, p. 279.
5. Bruce R. McConkie, *Mormon Doctrine, op. cit.,* p. 828.
6. Orson Pratt, *Journal of Discourses,* July 18, 1880, Vol. 21:288.
7. *Bible,* Revelations 12:4-9.
8. Bruce R. McConkie, *Mormon Doctrine, op. cit.,* p. 491.
9. *Bible,* Revelations 12:4-9.
10. Bruce R. McConkie, *Mormon Doctrine, op. cit.,* p. 828.
11. *Bible,* Revelations 12:7-9.
12. Hugh W. Nibley, "A Strange Thing in the Land" (Part 8), *The Ensign,* December, 1976, p. 73.
13. *Bible,* Revelations 12:7-9.
    Pearl of Great Price, Moses 6:49.
    Brigham Young, *Journal of Discourses,* Vol. 5:54-55.
14. *Ibid.*
15. Orson F. Whitney, "The Fall and the Redemption," *op. cit.,* p. 378.
16. Bruce R. McConkie, *Mormon Doctrine, op. cit.,* p. 828.
17. *Bible,* Matthew 12:30.
    Book of Mormon, 1 Nephi 14:10; Alma 5:38-40.

18. W. Cleon Skousen, "The Building Blocks of the Universe," *op. cit.,* p. 3.
19. Daniel H. Ludlow, *The Improvement Era, op. cit.,* p. 17.
20. Bruce R. McConkie, *Mormon Doctrine, op. cit.,* pp. 244-245.
21. See Chapter 3 of this book.
22. Orson Pratt, *Journal of Discourses,* July 18, 1880, Vol. 21:287.
23. *Ibid.*

Footnotes, Chapter Nine:

1. Bruce R. McConkie, *Mormon Doctrine, op. cit.,* p. 282.
2. Orson F. Whitney, "The Fall and the Redemption," *op. cit.,* p. 376.
3. Robert L. Millet, *Magnifying Priesthood Power, op. cit.,* pp. 40-41.
4. Orson Hyde, *Journal of Discourses,* October 6, 1859, Vol. 7:314-315.
5. *Ibid.*
6. Melvin J. Ballard, *The Three Degrees of Glory, op. cit.,* p. 21-22.
7. Duane S. Crowther, *Life Everlasting* (Bookcraft, Inc., Salt Lake City, Utah, 1967), pp. 38-44.
8. *The Instructor Magazine,* February, 1961, Vol. 96:40-41.

9. "The Pre-Mortality of Mankind," *The Relief Society Magazine,* September, 1970, Vol. 57:705.
10. Duane S. Crowther, *Life Everlasting, op. cit.,* pp. 539-540.
11. Joseph Fielding Smith, Jr., *The Improvement Era,* March, 1965, pp. 190-191.
12. *Ibid.*

Footnotes, Chapter Ten:

1. Bruce R. McConkie, *Mormon Doctrine, op. cit.,* p. 169.
2. Brigham Young, *Journal of Discourses,* April 9, 1852, Vol. 1:50.
3. W. Cleon Skousen, "A Working Memorandum on the Creation Story" (a non-classified article, of which a copy is presently in the possession of this author), pp. 1-11.
4. *Ibid.,* pp. 12-16.
5. R. Clayton Brough, *His Servants Speak* (Horizon Publishers, Bountiful, Utah, 1975), pp. 126-138.
6. W. Cleon Skousen, "A Working Memorandum on the Creation Story," *op. cit.,* pp. 12-16.
7. R. Clayton Brough, *His Servants Speak, op. cit.,* p. 133.

8. Orson Pratt, *Journal of Discourses,* November 12, 1876, Vol. 18:290.
9. Robert L. Millet, *Magnifying Priesthood Power, op. cit.,* pp. 36-37.
10. Melvin J. Ballard, *The Three Degrees of Glory,"* *op. cit.,* pp. 14-15.
11. Robert L. Millet, *Magnifying Priesthood Power, op. cit.,* pp. 36-37.

Footnotes, Chapter Eleven:

1. "A Uniform System for Teaching Investigators" (a missionary teaching plan and handbook, published by The Church of Jesus Christ of Latter-day Saints, August, 1968), p. 76.
2. Orson Pratt, *Journal of Discourses,* December 15, 1872, Vol. 15:244-245.
3. *Ibid.*
4. George Q. Cannon, *Journal of Discourses,* September 28, 1884, Vol. 26: 192-193.
5. Duane S. Crowther, *Life Everlasting, op. cit.,* pp. 16-17.
6. Orson Pratt, *Journal of Discourses,* December 15, 1872, Vol. 15:249-250.

Footnotes, Chapter Twelve:

1. See Chapter 10 of this book.

Brigham Young, *Journal of Discourses,* Vol. 3:319.
Orson Pratt, *Journal of Discourses,* Vol. 21:289.
2. Orson Pratt, *Journal of Discourses,* July 18, 1880, Vol. 21:289.
3. *Ibid.*
4. Brigham Young, *Journal of Discourses,* April 9, 1852, Vol. 1:50.
5. W. Cleon Skousen, "A Working Memorandum on the Creation Story," *op. cit.,* pp. 16-17.
6. *Ibid.*
7. Orson Pratt, *Journal of Discourses,* December 15, 1872, Vol. 15:25.
8. Bruce R. McConkie, *Mormon Doctrine, op. cit.,* pp. 290, 450.
9. *Ibid.*
Orson Pratt, *Journal of Discourses,* December 15, 1872, Vol. 15:251.
10. *Ibid.*
11. Bruce R. McConkie, *Mormon Doctrine, op. cit.,* p. 303.
12. James E. Talmage, *The Articles of Faith* (Deseret Book Company, Salt Lake City, Utah, 1967), p. 64.
13. *Pearl of Great Price,* Moses 2:27-28.
14. *Pearl of Great Price,* Moses 3:16-17.

Footnotes, Chapter Thirteen:

1. James E. Talmage, *The Articles of Faith* (Deseret

Book Company, Salt Lake City, Utah, 1967), p. 64.

2. *Ibid.,* pp. 64-65.
3. See Chapter 7 and 8 of this book.
   Orson Pratt, *Journal of Discourses,* November 22, 1873, Vol. 16:318.
4. R. Clayton Brough, "The Fall of Adam and Eve" (a college paper prepared for a religion class at B.Y.U. The original copy of the paper is in the possession of this author), 1972, pp. 1-4.
5. Orson Pratt, *Journal of Discourses,* November 22, 1873, Vol. 16:318.
6. R. Clayton Brough, "The Fall of Adam and Eve," *op. cit.,* pp. 3-4.
7. J. Preston Creer, "Fruits of the Fall," *op. cit.,* pp. 280-282.
8. *Orson Pratt,* Journal of *Discourses,* July 18, 1880, Vol. 21:288-289.
9. See Chapter 12 of this book.
10. James E. Talmage, *The Articles of Faith, op. cit.,* pp. 67-70.
11. *Ibid.*
12. *Ibid.,* p. 67.
13. See Chapter 10 of this book.
14. Bruce R. McConkie, *Mormon Doctrine, op. cit.,* pp. 17, 19-21.
15. Alma P. Burton, *Discourses of the Prophet Joseph Smith* (Deseret Book Company, Salt Lake City, Utah, 1956), p. 3.
16. Bruce R. McConkie, *Mormon Doctrine, op. cit.,* p. 21.
17. *Ibid.,* p. 18.
18. Orson Pratt, *Journal of Discourses,* July 18, 1880, Vol. 21:289-291.
19. *Ibid.*
20. *Ibid.*
21. Bruce R. McConkie, *Mormon Doctrine, op. cit.,* p. 401-402.

R. Clayton Brough, The Fall of Adam and Eve," *op. cit.,* pp. 3-4.

Selected Bibliography

Allred, Gordon, *Immortality* (Hawkes Publishers Inc., Salt Lake City, Utah, 1974), 416 pp.

Andrus, Hyrum L., *Doctrines of the Kingdom* (Bookcraft, Inc., Salt Lake City, Utah, 1973), 576 pp.

Ballard, Melvin J., *The Three Degrees of Glory* (Deseret Book Company, Salt Lake City, Utah, September 22, 1922), pp. 10-11.

Book of Mormon, The (The Church of Jesus Christ of Latter-day Saints, 1968 ed.), 568 pp.

Brigham Young University Speeches of the Year; Provo, Utah. An annual publication.

Brough, R. Clayton, *His Servants Speak* (Horizon Publishers, Bountiful, Utah, 1975), 298 pp.

Burton, Alma P., *Doctrines From the Prophets* (Bookcraft, Inc., Salt Lake City, Utah, 1970), 476 pp.

Church News (of The Church of Jesus Christ of Latter-day Saints), section of the Deseret News: a daily newspaper (Salt Lake City, Utah, 1943-1975).

Conference Reports (Annual and Semi-annual of the Church of Jesus Christ of Latter-day Saints, 1897-1975).

Crowther, Duane S., *Life Everlasting* (Bookcraft, Inc., Salt Lake City, Utah, 1967), 399 pp.

Doctrine and Covenants, The (The Church of Jesus Christ of Latter-day Saints, 1968 ed.), 312 pp.

Ensign, The (Monthly magazine of The Church of Jesus Christ of Latter-day Saints, 1970-1977).

First Presidency of The Church of Jesus Christ of Latter-day Saints, The, *Gospel Doctrine: Selections from the Sermons and Writings of Joseph F. Smith* (Deseret News Press, Salt Lake City, Utah, 1971), Volumes 1-2.

First Presidency of The Church of Jesus Christ of Latter-day Saints, The, *Immortality and Eternal Life: Selections from the Writings and Messages of President J. Reuben Clark, Jr.* (Deseret News Press, Salt Lake City, Utah, 1969), 388 pp.

Friend, The (Monthly magazine of the Church of Jesus Christ of Latter-day Saints, 1970-1977).

Gospel in Principle and Practice, The (Brigham Young University Press, Provo, Utah, 1966), Volumes 1-2.

Holy Bible, The (Old and New Testaments—King James Edition, Missionary copy bound for The Church of Jesus Christ of Latter-day Saints, 1969 ed.).

Improvement Era., The (Monthly magazine of The Church of Jesus Christ of Latter-day Saints, 1897-1970).

Inspired Version of the Bible (Reorganized Church of Jesus Christ of Latter-day Saints, Herald Publishing House, Independence, Missouri, 1944), 1,576 pp.

Instructor, The (Monthly magazine of The Church of Jesus Christ of Latter-day Saints, 1930-1970).

Journal of Discourses (Contains talks given by General Authorities and other Church leaders of the LDS Church between the years 1851-1886).

Juvenile Instructor (Monthly magazine of The Church of Jesus Christ of Latter-day Saints, 1866-1929).

Kimball, Spencer W., *The Miracle of Forgiveness* (Bookcraft, Inc., Salt Lake City, Utah, 1969), 376 pp.

Lee, Harold B., *Stand Ye In Holy Places* (Deseret Book Company, Salt Lake City, Utah, 1974), 398 pp.

McConkie, Bruce R., *Doctrines of Salvation: Sermons and Writings of Joseph Fielding Smith* (Bookcraft, Inc., Salt Lake City, Utah, 1954), Volumes 1-3.

McConkie, Bruce R., *Mormon Doctrine* (Bookcraft, Inc., Salt Lake City, Utah, 1966), 856 pp.

Millennial Star, The (Monthly magazine of The Church of Jesus Christ of Latter-day Saints, Great Britain, 1840-1970).

Millet, Robert L., *Magnifying Priesthood Power* (Horizon Publishers, Bountiful, Utah, 1974), 169 pp.

New Era, The (Monthly magazine of The Church of Jesus Christ of Latter-day Saints, 1970-1977).

Newquist, Jerreld L., *Gospel Truth: Discourses and Writings of President George Q. Cannon* (Deseret Book Company, Salt Lake City, Utah, 1957), Volumes 1-2.

Pearl of Great Price, The (The Church of Jesus Christ of Latter-day Saints, 1968 ed.), 65 pp.

Pratt, Orson, edited by, *The Seer* (Liverpool, England, 1853-1854), Volumes 1-2, 320 pp.

Pratt, Orson, *The Mormon Doctrine of Deity* (Horizon Publishers, Bountiful, Utah, 1974).

Relief Society Magazine, The (Monthly magazine of The Relief Society of The Church of Jesus Christ of Latter-day Saints, particularly 1914-1964).

Richard, Franklin D., and Little, James A., *A Compendium of the Doctrines of the Gospel* (1898 edition).

Richards, LeGrand, *A Marvelous Work and a Wonder* (Deseret Book Company, Salt Lake City, Utah, 1969 ed.), 452 pp.

Richards, LeGrand, *Israel, Do You Know* (Deseret Book Company, Salt Lake City, Utah, 1954), 252 pp.

Smith, Joseph (*The Documentary*) *History of the Church.* (Deseret Book Company, Salt Lake City, Utah, 1946-1951), Volumes 1-7.

Smith, Joseph F., *Gospel Doctrine* (Deseret Book Company, Salt Lake City, Utah, 1919), 553 pp.

Smith, Joseph Fielding, *Answers to Gospel Questions* (Deseret Book Company, Salt Lake City, Utah, 1957), Volumes 1-6.

Smith, Joseph Fielding, *Teachings of the Prophet Joseph Smith* Deseret News Press, Salt lake City, Utah, 1938), 408 pp.

Smith, Joseph Fielding, *The Progress of Man* (Genealogy Society, Salt Lake City, Utah, 1936), p.11

Talmage, James E., *Jesus The Christ* (Deseret Book Company, Salt Lake City, Utah, 1969 ed.), 804 pp.

Talmage, James E., *The Articles of Faith* (Deseret Book Company, Salt Lake City, Utah,1961 ed.), 536 pp.

Teachings of the Living Prophets (Brigham Young University Press, Provo, Utah, 1970), 323 pp.

Widtsoe, John A., *Discourses of Brigham Young* (Deseret Book Company, Salt Lake City, Utah, 1954), 497 pp.

Index

O

Organized Intelligences, see "Spirit Children"
Order of the Gods, 37-40.

P

Parents, some pre-mortal spirits able to choose their mortal parents, 94-95.
Physical Deformities, in mortality, are not related to some pre-mortal punishment, 102-104.
Plants, all have spirits, 126.
Power, of our Father in Heaven accorded Him by the righteous intelligence of the universe, 44-47.
Pratt, Orson, 27, 40-41, 42-43, 50, 52-53, 56, 57-58, 61-62, 75, 79, 82-83, 88-89, 133-135, 136-137, 139-140, 147-148, 155-156.
Pratt, Parley P., 64.
Pre-Earthly Existence, the meaning and proper use of term, 13-14.
Pre-Existence, improper use of term, 13-14.
Predestination, is not foreordination, 70-71.
Pre-Mortal Existence, importance of learning about, 20-24; knowledge of helps us to maintain a righteous and happy manner while in mortality, 22; knowledge of, helps us to understand joy, pain, good and evil, 20-24; meaning and proper use of term, 13-14; our, characteristics are brought with us into mortality, 100-102; remembrance of, will return to us after death, 136-137; ancient and modern scriptural evidences of, 14-20; stories of people seeing a remembering events of the pre-mortal life, 94-100; understanding the, can maintain or restore an individuals self-respect, 22-24; why modern Christianity does not accept the doctrine of, today, 17-20.
Priesthood, why Negroes cannot hold the priesthood today, 93-94.

R

Roberts, Brigham H., 50.

S

Salvation, plan of, accepted in the Council in Heaven, 76-80.

Satan, and his evil followers cast out of God's presence, 82-89; and his rebellious followers cast out of Heaven and down to earth, 84-89; drew away one third of the spirit hosts of heaven designed for this earth to rebel against their God, 82; entered into a beast called a serpent in the Garden of Eden to tempt Eve, 145-146; justification for Satan and his followers being cast down from heaven without the possibility of ever obtaining bodies, 86-89; leads a third of the spirit hosts of heaven to war against God, 81; perhaps not the first evil spirit to rebel against Deity, 88-89; proposed a plan of "forced redemption" without free-agency, 79-80; see also "Devil" and "Lucifer."
Scriptures, evidences in the, of the pre-mortal existence of man, 14-17.
Second Estate, is mortality, 91.
Sill, Sterling W., 53.
Skousen, W. Cleon, 27-33, 39-40, 44-47, 86, 106-119, 141, 142.
Smith, Joseph, 25-26, 37-38, 40, 42, 59-60, 74.
Solar System, Abraham knew ours, was 2/3 out from the center of our Galaxy.
Sons of God, shout for joy when God laid the foundations of this earth, 75.
Spirit Bodies, limitations of our, 54-55; specific nature of our, 53-54.
Spirit Element, see "Intelligence."
Spirits, no neutral spirits during the war in heaven, 85-86; our, in the form of our mortal bodies, 52-54; similarities and relationships to matter and intelligence, 34-36; some pre-mortal, were able to choose their mortal parents, 94-95; some progressed further in premortality than did others, 62-64; we were all, offspring of our Father in Heaven, 49-56.
Spiritual Birth, literal nature of our, 50-52.
Spirit Children, as, of our Eternal Father and Mother in Heaven we were begotten spiritually, 51-52; referred to as "organized intelligences," 33-34; as, we were entities similar in form to our mortal bodies, 34.